JINZHOU

KYOTO

BALTIMORE

# JINZHOU
# KYOTO
# BALTIMORE

## POEMS
*New and Selected*

**Scott Francis**

Loom Press
Amesbury, Massachusetts
2024

*Jinzhou, Kyoto, Baltimore: Poems New and Selected*


The character on the cover is called *shi*, meaning poem or poet.

ISBN 978-0-931507-46-5

Published in the United States of America
First Edition

Design: Keith Finch with Ashley Rosario
Font: Alternate Gothic and Merriweather
Author photograph: Sonne Studios
Printing: Versa Press, Illinois

Loom Press
15 Atlantic View, Amesbury, MA 01913
www.loompress.com
info@loompress.com

—for Irene

# Contents

# NEW POEMS

# *from* Homage to Emily Dickinson

Having taken some ten years to complete *The Ice Storm* and another year editing tanka written in 2004, in order to create *Wilderness*, I was looking for something new to write. I happened to glimpse my battered, disintegrating copy of Emily Dickinson's poems. It was my third copy of her work, having destroyed through use during my lifetime two other hardcover editions. A thought occurred to me. Maybe after all these decades of writing I have attained skill enough to just go ahead and directly copy Dickinson's formal technique and yet create something worthwhile.

I only dared because of a synchronicity. I had attended a wedding near Springfield, MA, Dickinson's home and site of her grave. After the wedding, before beginning the six-hour drive home, I drove to her grave, intending to visit. A thunderstorm, viciously unrelenting and seemingly forever, made me drive by without paying homage to her. The words "Because I could not stop for Emily she kindly said to me—" popped into my consciousness and this phrase kept on coming back to me, along with the memory of the thunderstorm.

I am really getting too old to care what people think about my writing, unless the thoughts are more than pejorative. I am going ahead with a book titled *Homage to Emily Dickinson*. Like Dickinson's *Collected*, it is arranged in the order written and has no single unifying theme or subject. It is simply the spontaneous outflowing of a poet reacting to his experience. In this way the unifying theme and subject is the poet's self, and by extension the book presents the self, Coleridge's the great I am. Many words and phrases are taken from Dickinson as outlined in the notes, but always used in ways unique to the poem at hand. Nothing is simply lifted.

# A Violent Thunderstorm Forced Me to Drive Right By Emily Dickinson's Gravestone

Because I could not stop for Emily—
She kindly said to me—
"Your car holds nothing but yourself
And immortality."

I slowly drove—I knew no haste—
Lightning gleamed off her stone—
Thunder announced—why—the word—
"Dickinson" means alone

When death arrives—"When thy time comes—
Look to my hybla balms—
My dews of Thessaly—you'll—fetch
Off the shelf, many psalms—"

We passed a school, where Covid hit
And recess knew no posy
Of rings around a new Black Death
Where all fall down, rosie.

"You, like I, know what passion means
When boundaries of pain
Soar away and—we—dare—to smite
Gabriel's wings with flame—"

We passed a hospital like souls
Entering doors of—light—
Where valves had heart—enough—to walk
Upstairs to—Paradise—

We passed a funeral home. "For sale,"
The sign declared—Not wealth
Enough to make ceremony worth—
Man's—time—

"I wanted warmth to undress me—
My garter was of gold—
Virginity's dusk—my blood's—dark
Beyond pain to—unfold—

"Essential oils to massage me
When attar of the rose
Makes summer of an empty room
And rosemary—love's ruse—

"Who could have been my suitors—gone—
I was no slave to death
Jailed within my dear brother's home—
Free—when I wrote—

"Oceans of tides—the new moon's rise—
Gravity's pull—love's tears
When shores flood out and wharves, destroyed—
Each wave rends—Love rips, tears—

"When we learn why the wind's a pathos
Of individual voice
Beyond ourselves—when—all—of what
The quiet is—no choice

"But to become a consciousness
Prone to—discovery—
Intrepid, an adventurer
Alone—to really see—"

We passed a light—It was not green—
It was not red—Cut off—
Devoid of energy—no light—
Utility—aloft—

Deluge erupted. I pulled over—
Switched on the radiance
Scarlet—Emergencies of light—
Each blink beheld—Wounds dance—

"For only gossamer, my gown—
My tippet—only tulle—
Whatever of my bones in dirt
Is holy—I—can't tell—"

Into the entranceway I could not turn—
The lightning wrote a—code—
Of messages gone flick and—blank—
Too hard for me to read—

Unable to decipher why
I surmised my car hood's
Horizons stretched—exactly—like
Emily's horses' heads—

## For Flaco, The Central Park Zoo's Eagle Owl Escapee

Feathered horns, with whoosh and the fury
Of flight unfurled from cage
And zoo tame boredom, the death stare
And plummet,  hunger's rage

Erupts from its dusk flyouts with
Talons floating down
To infestations and a rat
Nabbed to gobble, beak doom

Soaring onto an oak limb
To gorge upon the meal
And hang out, satisfaction gained,
Dinner, a raw, good deal

Whose remains, balls of bone and fur
Vomited up, feed
All of Manhattan's cameras
With wild celebrity,

Proof that wise instinct's owlish brains
Can hunt, untaught, the free
Hidden by day, a moonlit glimpse
Overhead, shadowy—

Flaco thrives, testament and sign,
Proof of the wilderness
Central, the wilder park and scowl
Bless-ed, who feasts in bliss,

Born to transcend a city fate
Of lockdowns and dead food
Cold, a destiny of eats

Good and fresh. Let a brood
Female escape and many young
To be a mating blest
By plenty and love's bounty sure
In hatchlings and a nest

Of owlet futures and some good
Investments for the soul
To feed and grow, a profit for
Dawn watchers who'll behold

Freedom in leaves and the central dark
Upbraiding prisons with
A hoot more than a hoot, pure song
Decrying liberty no myth.

## The Ancient Romans Believed Souls Ride Dolphins to the Isles of Paradise

—for Emily Dickinson (Cf. ED #818, "The Thoughtfulness of Thirst")

She earned an afterlife of fame
By jotting down unknown
Songs written out in thoughtfulness
When she found time alone

To take up a pen, finding far
Geographies within
Where shores and whole Atlantics vast
Slaked her thirst. Her myth is

Oceans of dolphins and the leap
Of dorsal fins, the whirl
Up through wave after wave on toward
Isles of an inner world

Where spray and salt and the foam's lash
Whipped her up through the seas
Colder than time, the tidal pull,
Art's immortality—

Thought and thirst, lightning in the surge
Up on the dolphin's back
Piercing the typhoon's eye to find
Calm within the wrack—

Thought and thirst, the cling to the warmth
Of ocean mammal blood
In pulse where reaches and the depths
In currents heal the bled—

Thought and thirst, tortured lifelong needs
For faith and certainty
Compelling intuitions of a
Tragic eternity—

Upon her dolphin she—departed—
To the Isles as she passed
With a drawerful of poems to her
Name, her writing pressed

Like autumn leaves in books, each leaf
To be discovered hurling
Soul on up the fury and the swell
Of hurricanes unfurling

Beyond the fear of drowning. There's
A dolphin to be ridden
When she appears and signals with
A leap of Isles—unbidden—

An offering, a calling's echo,
Cliffs full of gull cries, depths
Of shores where an interior
Beckons beyond death—

To be found by a consciousness
Without the need for fame,
One making the Isles, unknown, known
By giving them a name.

## Frailty

(Reply to Dickinson's #822)

Snarls growl hard and the hunger's glare,
Pouncing, leaps to the chase,
Sniffs out the wounded, my own self
It feasts upon.  The race

Plays out on paws and hurls so far
That I erupt and bound
Into the wilderness, identity,
My own, the single hound

Who barks at neighbors and the sun
As if my whine by door
And fence could allow me to be
Spared the attacks of dear,

Old wild desire, coyote fangs
Slavering to seek
Out the hound and close in when the
Dog's alone, old and weak,

Forgotten, left out every night
As if neglect could feed
Whatever unmet wants a pet
Dies for. I'm saved by greed

For true experience between
My intervals of death
And re-creation, consciousness,
Mine, an experiment

Appointed unto me when a
Pack of coyotes nose
Open the unlocked backyard door—
For all my yelps they close

In but the self can't understand
Nor accept its own death
And so I gain another self
Even as I die, dragged

Away by hunger, silence un-
Acknowledged but aware
Of hunger's rip. Appetites, raw,
What consciousness must fear,

What I become, an animal
Unaware of death,
Invasive, of a species now
Found everywhere, the scents

Of murder, the coyote crouched,
Camouflaged by some wheel
Or shadow underneath some car—
Unseen, denied. Fangs whirl.

They lunge. Cascading desire, fear,
The wilderness of slums
Called affluence, my home, its haunt
And hunting ground. It looms,

Devoid of all morality,
A new identity
Beyond myself, myself become
Itself condemned to be

Nothing but itself.

## For a Scientist Present at the Experiment

—Commemorating the December 2022 Nuclear Fusion Breakthrough

Radiance ignites and a star
Mirrors in goggles pressed
To keep the retinae unblind
In witness of the burst

In billionths of a second and
Genius. She eyes the star
Plasma and an archangel's cry
Unfolds out of her stare

Taking in the light of so much
Energy, a brain
Synapsed beyond all knowledge, the
Divine, the anti-hate

And a solution, a beginning
When sand dunes sands Kitty Hawk
Jump and brothers, in brotherhood, take flight—
To make up for much loss.

Ideality, becoming real.

# *from* Wilderness

My wife and I left Kyoto in early spring, 2004. We returned home to the United States, starting new lives, taking a year off before beginning anew. For eight months, equipped with a tent, a tarp, a cooler, a camp stove and a small car, we camped throughout the southwestern and northwestern mountains, shores and deserts. At times, we reconnected with family and old friends. Memories of these experiences inspire these poems.

Japan's delight in the miniature informs these poems. Their point of departure begins with such arts as haiku, bonsai and netsuke.

# Moth

Confusions of the radiance
By nature, reduced to idiocy
Fatal, the misunderstanding

Lucifer, the morning star,
draws up in orbit It brightens approaching day

The moth flutters, floating into the candleflame

Wings of char
unfold Lucifer, the morning star
The devil may care Nothing but an insect's stare

No, this is not the persistence of evil
No, this is not the forgetfulness, the disremembrance

This is being burned, a flit crisped

The antennae singe
off Torn from Heaven's songs,
Lucifer, the morning star,

burns Taken by the candleflame, the moth,
ablaze,

drops

## On Sleeping in Juan Delgado's Library

Lorca's soul haunts the broken
spines Many, many books reread many times,
battered by a

rush
of hands

Decades' reaching, reading

Lorca's skull haunts the
top shelf Long ago shot by fascists,
weeping dust, the eye pits see

what they can
see

Outside, a nightjar shrieks

Lorca, the starlit
mountainside He haunts the empty
chair

For hours, turning pages,
he's reading what the living have to bear

Words formed in the song and presence of his trust

## Late Night Desert Cougar Attack

—Desert Oasis, Eastern Oregon, Malheur NWR

Like wheels, whimpering
squeals Like thought, blood
reels Eruptions of lungs cry out

The racoon
shrieks

Not a quick, but a long bitten down death

The fangs bare a
universe The jaws chew down the
galaxies The meal's attributes cannot be caused by mere creation

Played with, clawed, the racoon
has no need for metaphysics

Always hungry, necessity licks its chops

The night sky's a
river of sums Equations stream,
multiplying into the Milky Way's irreducible calculus

Inexpressible solutions expand into time's
star-like

endlessness

## In Defense of a Rain Forest Slug

—Vancouver Island

Slander to call it
slimy     Slippery, it slides,
slick     Though it's never too slick

Sluggish?
More slander

Touching, untouched

Slipshod, the sole
slips     The stumble
stomps the

shell-
less soul

Love flees this broken world

Done
writhing, the horns on stalks
collapse

Swarmed over by ants
No grave will mark this desecration

The soul!  The sole's to blame

## On Global Warming

No, not a crash, lightning-like, of
Antarctic icecaps drowning us all but a
Medieval, slow

    downward spiral        Where nights are a
        vial of antidepressants

A psychiatric dark

Stupidity, we,
Medieval        God knows, we've evolved
from star explosions        The stuff of novas, we are

        what we are
    For our children, this

For our children's children, this

    By the billions, we
struggle        Each yearning, churning,
worming        Scurrying

        bacteria        Encephalitic, replicating
    prions        Particles of Covid

We

## Grasshopper

—in Smith River, Redwoods NRA

A shrike flicks to
feast      My long legs blinkleap wink
away

I've escaped into the
azure

sky

My flit's fluttering floats to an
angel's palm      My grip electrifies the
being feeling how I'm a

wilderness of power,
an engine of escape

I'm as dazzling as the azure sky

How doth my blinkleap
echo? Like a thief in the night,
a rustling away, a whispering of

escape
I

am I      I am the azure sky

## Venus So Large It Casts Shadows

—Gila National Forest, NM

Venus metal,
molten     The planet pours into the
crucible, oak and holly twigs

An
oasis tangle

Your skin

Venus tangle, your
gaze     Blaze melts within the
crucible, oak and holly twigs

Mettle of
planet metal

Your skin

Venus gaze,
deluge     Molten floods the
crucible, oak and holly twigs

The
radiance

Your skin

## Easter Sunrise Among the Sangre de Christo Mountains

—Near Taos, NM

Thunderously, a
lizard flicks        Christ's sky delivers blood to the
desert ranges

Out of a cave hole
Up from Hell

Arisen

Horns,
a copper stare        Zinc's turquoise,
the lizard blinks

Christ strolls up the crags of blood
He climbs the many folds on folds torn by thirst and wounds

He's brightening the summits

Horns
ablaze        Spikes of flames, a
conflagration

Platinum, the eyelids
Thorns, the spine

The lizard basks, reddened by Easter's sun

## Ode to a Chipmunk

—Sequoia National Forest

Confucius perched up on
hind legs, you sniff
You sneeze

In query
A question mark

Quaking

Those who think they know
know not        Those who think they know not,
know, I think        O,

Confucius,
what knows your nose?

You sneeze

Braveheart,
your swerve and whirl
lifes alive pure

beauty
The very fact of you astounds

Grace abounds

## An Allen's Hummingbird

—Northern California Coast

Flames in the azure
eye of God, conflagrations lighting up the
sky, a burning visionary,

I My spangling
winks

Dangling, I'm a harlequin of fire

Laughter's
retina of God, zings winged in
razzmatazz, zap zip jazz

dangling,
syncopations spangling,

I, the harlequin, riff alive a newfound flower chord

A joker of fireworks, I'm
spangling Laughter's azure,
dangling, with zipzapzings

to the flower I fling
I sip up the feast

I am delight's beast

# The Javelina

—Scottsdale, AZ

Ballerina, boar,
no ham    Haunch by hoof joint,
tiptoeng on point

Arizona suburbs provide the stage
You trot alive our desert age

Your grand plié plots, invading homeowner plots

To prance even goddesses
need feast    Your snout snorts, tusked
You rut tulip bulbs up

You
munch

I've a hunch you'll stay for lunch

Trembling, your bristles
sniff Man    Your mug puffs up, bluffs a
five-hundred pound porker's snort

Your scowl's the rex
in Arizona's tyrannosaurus

Dwarf pigs?  As pretty as they please

# A Black-and-White Moth Flutters From Rain Forest Last Light

—Washington State, Olympia National Park

Onyx
murk        Pearl
night

Antennaed well,
you sense the scents of the future's sense

Onto my palm you float

O, onyx
O, pearl    Your fragility tells me death is
beauty's price

Puff up your antennae
Read my palm

Prophecy

Onyx, pearl my
psalms       Question my
palm

Gypsy,
fib if you be true

Whisper of immortality

## Belated Love Poem

—Wenatchee National Forest, Washington State

Forgive me        Time
has died        No love poem razzmatazz
jazzes us this morning

Frost in mint, the dawn's
touch

Snow among many crevices and rivers

Mint
frost        The first rays
provide no heat

Too much has been lost to time
Forgive me

It is snowing

Breakfast among the
wild mint        Coffee to assuage our
frozen bones        It's time

We can't stop it
The mountains' snowline is descending

We have to go

## North Cascades National Park, May River

Chalky, glacial
run off        Boney, ground down
mountains

Rapids, rumbling away
Death's thundering on

The slurry of the gone

Colder than Antarctica, the
rapids hurl up like
trucks

The dead won't go quietly
They're thundering on

The cries of the gone

Warmth
shatters apart the glacial rifts
Collapsing into avalanche, the ice cliffs

Skulls, skeletons of mountains,
the rapids crunch, cracking and splintering

The music of the gone

## Mojave Desert A.M.

Raw, the blade
Naked, the unbled
Rising, the blood

scythe
knifes the dark out of the dark

The crescent moon, dawning, reddens the arroyos and the hoodoos

Love's a
heart attack hammering within an
antelope chased so long and hard it falls in a crash of horns and hooves

Coyotes gang
Squabbling, each fang

The devouring delivers death's harangue

A skull
frowns With dry skill,
the fangs scowl

Coyote bones
thinking hard, they're wondering what they are

They have no answer

## In Praise of Autumn

—High Desert Oasis, Malheur National Wildlife Refuge

Raven, shrike,
coyote fang pink
reeds          Hunger, mirroring

A riverside gorged with seeds
A watery ashen bittern sparrow chaos

Beauty laughs, knowing it fulfills all needs

All but the browns
brown out          Leather sulfur oriole
rippling

A
foal-blue husk

A yellowthroat erupts into melody

Minerals azurite and
copper     Skeletal, on fire
Lizard hazel zinc

Marrow, the currents
Platinum, the shores

Everything, even death has gone to seed

## Beetle

An underworld's glance,
a devil's face        Horned, suffering a shadowy verdict
Guilty of life, condemned to a slow death

On its back
Belly up is a cruel and unusual punishment

It is a maze of endless formal beauty

Each eye's
many eyes        Cathedral windows, shattered
A shell        A sanctuary, war-battered

Unable
to seek and find

No one will ever know what flits through a dying beetle's mind

Automatic protoplasm
A head, an abdomen, a thorax
As nature and time demand, the antennae act

They spasm
Their shadows collapse and flick back up out of bottomless calamity

An exoskeleton, exposed on a granite slab

# Raven Glimpsed in the Getty Museum's Japanese Garden

Universe of no
death No death
invades the temple grounds

Its flight resounds
It abounds

The hooded negative

It soars by a
bamboo grove The wings loom up the
raked temple sands

It resounds
Each feather, diamond-like, abounds

The hooded negative

Chromatic,
crystalline Love's diamond ground
The wings resound

They abound,
meaning more than the sand designs

The hooded negative

# *from* Baltimore (2011–2021)

# Isaiah

"Isaiah" is the tale of a ten-year-old confronting the truths of his uncle killed in Vietnam. The poem arises directly from my personal experience. From 1965 to 1967, my parents took in a foster child and helped him graduate from high school. Against my father's strongest wishes, he left college, enlisted as a second lieutenant and went to Vietnam. A year later he was slain, when I was ten and had all the affection of a younger brother for the man. In 1986, I happened to meet a Vietnam veteran. I described some specifics of the death, such as the cause of death listed as "death by friendly fire," the reported condition of the remains and the unopened casket. The veteran put his hand to my skull and mimed a gun firing, saying, "Fragged." He went on to explain the epidemic of fragging that went on towards the end of the Vietnam conflict. In 2010, I visited Washington, D.C., visited the Vietnam Veterans Memorial and located my foster brother's name. Fragging is draftees murdering officers to avoid combat. This tragedy is well documented by both government documents and by personal testimony, much of which is found on the internet.

## Isaiah

Alone,
Isaiah runs up to his window, wipes it clean
And stares out at lands possessed by the Winter King.
Everywhere reveals realms of castles locked in ice.
Driveway drawbridges near and far span moats of ice.
Gargoyle guards stand sentry on far glacial heights.
Death's fortress battlements and turrets tower like
The mountain ranges of Antarctica. Love's plight,
Windows of eyes, a lady longs to find the knight
Who'll free her from her tower ensorcelled in ice.
To be Sir Galahad, Excalibur become his sword
Bashing to batter down the lady's blizzard lord,
Who blights the land with ice and urges all to war.
The Winter King charges on Cheerless, his ice horse.
On Good, Sir Galahad, headlong, hurls in, love's force.
Neighs shriek. Hooves lash. Blood erupts in Good's face.
The Winter King fangs, "I bring famine. You I waste."
His sword thunders on down. Death's lord of lords
Yelps as his sword clangs back, met by the sword of swords,
Excalibur. The blade's thrustthrash thwack stabs the King.
The tyrant shrivels up in flames. Away his ashes fling.
The white rose lady, freed, petals in her every look,
Rides up to Galahad, a red rose in her look.
To go outside and play alive the stories in his book.
His only friend, Stump, the dwarf, yells, "Woe! Olden woe.
Woefully wander wastrels bloodied by blood blasts to know."
"What does that mean?" "I know you know I know you know."
"What's wrong with you?" "What is wrong with who? Do not dare."
Out of the floorboards the dwarf leaps up, "I said, 'Do not dare.'"
"Don't dare what?" "Venture not outside." "Why not?" "You fool,
Wolves are the lightning's flingdrool fanging down to devour you.
Flee their flashblip growllash zip snap snouts thundering where
Our backyard used to be." "But I can't see them." "Everywhere
They bound out of the ice storm's blabtruth blast blam blear."

"That's not what I see." "You're blind." "I behold a court of ice.
It's hosting a world tournament of lightning-armored knights
Aglitter as they boom, jousting here, there, to win the white
Rose lady. She sobs, having to choose one who'll bound
Onward to slay the Winter King." A tale like in his book,
A darkling's shadow shudders. The shame's eyebeams rake
Up, down the lady. She pretends not to behold his look.
"I have to go and save her." "But that's only in your book."
"Shut up, Stump." Lightning leaves a wound.
It stabs the sap down to the pith. The old oak swoons.
The backyard sick tree earthquakes down. "It's lightning struck."
The house shakes like God's blacksmith blasts a hammer strike
Out-thundering thunder, making a sword of such lightning strength
The anvil cracks. The tree collapses down the breadth and length
Of wires torn out and the transformers trashed. Like love on fire,
Like a girl napalmed, spangling, a blaze crying out on her scarred life,
The branches, dangling, splutterspark. They spurt. Like blood.
Like Vietnam left Uncle dead. Ice storm dark darts in. "Out?
Stump, tell me. Is it true? Have all the lights blinked out?"
Stump runs up about, swatting switches. "They're all out."
In its death throes the dragon oak claws sparks of jewels
Out of the wires. "Treasure. . ." "The wealth's a gift for fools."
"But it's a hoard of rubies for my white rose lady.
To her I'll bow and cry, 'Jewels enough to sate thee,
Tender rose.'" Stump rolls his eyes like they're Ferris wheels.
"Tender rose?" "Yup." "A fool for romance learns to scream."
"What?" "Go not out. Your death will make your parents grieve."
"It will not." "It will." "Mom and dad care about work, not me."
"Even the heartiest of heroes can know nothing of immortality.
Go not out." "Why not?" "The wires, fool. They are live." "We'll see."
Stump scowls, scurries up, grabs and tugs hard at the boots
Isaiah struggles to put on. Stump's tough old finger roots
Run up the laces, knotting the knots not. Kicks him away.
"You're only make believe." "So you say. You, not I, will pay."
Isaiah swings wide the door. "Death is not child's play.
Out there electrocution pops the eyeballs to a fizz
Like soda." "Yeah, I know. But I am no wimp." "You stay in."
"Nope." "You will die." "I don't care." Stump pulls at his coat.

He slaps him away, steps out and confronts oiled oceans cold,
Arctic shores and death's ice infinity. "Go back in." Slips,
Cannot catch at the railing, cries out, "Father," flips,
Smashes down off the backyard deck steps all
Alone. He slides on down the ice rink lawn
Facedown. It's gravity grinding his face
In. Or it's entropy, the force,
The maelstrom star
Sea
Whirlpool
None can see,
The black hole center of our galaxy.
Isaiah up and wrote a twenty-five page paper about it.
The boy attached a comprehensive, trillion site e-bibliography.
Skies on skies of cloud memory could not hold all of his appendices.
His study told him that an object falling into a black hole—
Called gravitational time dilation—makes time seem to slow
As if it takes forever to plummet down into the black hole.
The ice storm spatterclicks, ticking time's tock slop seep
Down Isaiah's neck. Nothing but a Greenland ice cap creep
Gone splatdrip plip plop down his back like sweat to weep
Whole worlds warm. Nothing's broken, staggers up to slip
Treasure out of the dragon oak's guts lightning split
In two. "Ba-back off," wimps out Stump, "I've got to piss
For fear." Isaiah giggles. The oak's ripped wires hissspit
Roar and spark up tongue flames flicked to guard what is its
By right of theft and mayhem. Greed, the dragon, the old sin,
Feints a charge, starting back. "It is," Stump shrieks, "Alive.
One touch and you'll be donuts deep fried on high. Go inside."
"Obey your coward thing," the dragon says, "Boy, go inside."
"You dare infest my yard, worm? Say your prayers. You die."
The dragon guffaws, nostrils snorting snot and lightning bolts.
"On my sword you will learn to squirm." "You dolt of dolts,
My breath's more than ninety-nine megabillion murder volts.
You drip in dirty diapers, you tot tottering, flee or you will die."
"Nope." "Chubby Chortle, Tubby Chump, go home and cry."
The dragon dares galaxy a black hole. "Gosh." Lo, its breath
H-bomb erupts like the Gulf Sea oil deck. The wreck

Vomited oil on down the Mississippi shores forever.
The birds, slimed, and the flounder, floundering, never
Stopped flopping out of oil wave after wave. "Inept,
Typically corporate. O, son—" Dad's tears spurt. Down they crept.
He and Isaiah stared at the TV. "What more can we expect?
An ingrained bureaucratic elite, son—" Shores of death.
Rats multiplied like humans. The mass fed on death.
Maggots and beetles feasted on the ocean's dearth.
Bulldozer blades bit in, plowing rot and the shore
Under like bullshit plows truth under, like a war
Covers up the truth. Ice twigs clip Isaiah's face.
Ice branches rip his bruised, his bashed blue face
As into the collapsed oak he runs to play all day.
Into the dragon's roar the knight screams on to slay
Vomit fireball explosions and the oil deck's flack,
The impact of pollution denied and each, every fact,
Like Vietnam killed Uncle, his kids unborn, left no trace,
No cousins ever to befriend, Thanksgiving with no trace—
Christmas afternoons alone—Mom and Dad up in bed—
When their son can only play pretend—cousins, dead—
Asking to see their presents, making up their names,
To join in on the fun, to play the funnest of their games,
But nothing's in games when the unborn bear no names.
Naming, death chiseled away at the black hole's antishimmer.
Death chipped namelessness out of the wall's granite glitter.
At first no names reflected from the polish and the depths
As the walk down mirrored Isaiah's family like death
Laughs at those who believe the dead are really dead.
Fifty-eight thousand names cried out on their death.
Most, if not slain, would now be among the undead.
Each had grief and tales of life's ecstasies to tell.
They reflected the boy's walk down to Uncle's hole,
The center of the galaxy, where the stars maelstrom down
Into the black hole supermassive. Doom! It is our doom.
Lightlessness will grip our burnt out sun and drag it on down
In. Dad grabbed Isaiah's hand and would not let him go.
"There's nothing to fear, son." The child saw his uncle's name.
Dad dragged his son up to the letters of the boy's own name.

"Your uncle is your namesake," Dad said, "See? Your name."
Along with Mom and Dad Isaiah studied his own name.
The letters blurred back and revealed the blackest hole,
Uncle's face torn by war. The face rose out of the hole.
Uncle bushwhacked up and out,
Whole.
He put his face up to Isaiah's. He grabbed the child's hand.
"Uncle reached out, snatched my hand and yanked it so hard
My arm, like, fell off." "Forgive him. War leaves men scarred."
"You saw how he pulled me." "A tug of war. You—" "Fell.
Yes, I fell—" "Into the black hole." "I did not want to fall.
Stump, you saw how I held on." "You could not help but fall."
"I hit bottom hard." "In dawn jungle." "It was really cold."
"Wet." "A swamp." "Fields of emerald beyond." "Blest, not damned."
"Uncle showed you how he died." "He had to command."
"The platoon he led—" "But, he did. He bravely led."
"From behind, one of his men shot him through the head."
In drips of tears Isaiah and Stump go back to their game
Of battling dragon flames to achieve white rose fame
But being alone, always alone again. It's gone lame.
The stories themselves yawn and admit they are lame.
Dragons? No, not again. The same old same old same.
Isaiah's read the Bible on the sly. His folks would freak
If they knew their son had religion. Dad snarled, "Fuck
God, even if there is one." When the boy Isaiah found
Prophet Isaiah in the Bible, his blood thrilled aloud,
Heart's pitterpat and boom—his own name, wow—
Until he read it. Here was some old huff
Full of predictions, pretty boring stuff
Except where Lucifer, the morning star, fell,
Cast out of Heaven, his wings on fire, the prince of Hell,
An angel like an H-bomb mushrooms up. His fall
Lit up the world's dawn. "He hit Earth so hard his yell,
To this day, can be heard." "Must be we've gone to Hell."
"Like that sound?" "What sound?" "That, like something's dead."
"That's loneliness realizing what the living cannot bear to dread."
"To me it sounds like wolves." "The pack runs?" "It is on the prowl."
"They're getting nearer." "Animals—" "Hear how they growl."

"The engine's turning up the street." "It's hurtling in to slay."
"Fangs of red, tongues of wheels awhirl—" "They eat child prey."
Fire truck doors open. Multitudes of wolves leap out.
"Stump, what can I do?" "Call on Uncle." "But, he's dead."
"Don't be an idiot." "Uncle?" "Yes?" "Help me or I'm dead."
As the wolves bound in, bullets blast brain bones and blood.
The center of the head. Uncle snipes the wolves dead.
Worldwide wounds waterfall and star brains leak out.
The brains defy the black hole's pull. Starlight ekes out.
Those wolves still alive flee up the lawn's spangled gleam
Of rubies twinkling, sapphires, stars, a white rose sheen,
Blood chalcedony, diamonds azure, pearls wild, clean,
Not scarlet scarring battlefields, but the whiteblue, clean,
Not scarlet shattered into multiplicities of wounded light,
Not trees and shrubs and lawns discolored by the siren lights.
Rumors claim it's Christ stealing up like a thief in the night.
"YOU ARE, KID, INCHES FROM A LIVE WIRE." "What is that?"
"KID, DON'T MOVE." "Stump, is it true?" "You fool." "What?"
"KID, LISTEN TO ME." "But there is the Winter King."
"You are a fool." "But, it is. It's the Winter King."
Armored in sable and gold, a wolf thing
Reaches out gauntlets, its big eye
Within its forehead,
Its helmet eye—
"DON'T MOVE. PLEASE, KID. DON'T. YOU WILL DIE."
"He's trying to catch me. Hide, Stump. O, hide. Hide."
He snowmobiles it out of there. Matched stride for stride—
Galaxy whirlpool star claws take him and his dwarf alive.
"KID, CALM DOWN." The child, thrashing, hears his dad
Talk. Was last year, after their walk down to the dead
Of Vietnam. Mom's, "But it has been decades, love.
Can't you put your grief away?" "My grief honors him."
Dad's tears tornadoed. Mom's, "So many tears? Now?"
They hugged, ignored Isaiah. "But I've never told you how—"
Their voices fell. Isaiah heard it all though Stump
Covered his ears. "Don't listen," hissed the grump.
"His own men," Dad said, "Put a bullet through his head.
Fragging, that's when the men don't obey, but, instead,

Shoot down their officers. A rash of it at the war's end.
Look it up. Brother, he's out in front. Brave. Him. See.
He does his duty, leads. 'We're going in,' he has to say.
He turns to lead. From behind, one pop pops his head."
The tears fell like stars. "But he wanted kids. He's dead.
I'll never be there for his kids. My brother's dead. He's dead."
"Only you and I, Stump, know Uncle pulled me into Vietnam
And showed me how he ended in a bullet's blood blast blam
BEFORE Dad told Mom about it." "That's the truth." Lies
Are not Isaiah's to believe. Dragged by the King, he writhes.
Arms pinned, screams, tries to bite. Shut in the house,
Victorian, where the ghost haunting the walls, Uncle Mouse,
Skitters for crumbs, the child has to unbait the kitchen traps.
Traps frag skulls. "You think you're so good?" Stump yaps,
"You must fulfill your duty or you know your mom and dad—"
Up on a kitchen chair the fireman props Isaiah like
The boy's a doll. "Do you mind, sir, if I start to do my
Homework?" "Not without a light. Would be bad for your
Eyes." Stump fires up a candle. "Well, then, it's okay."
Rage
To be more than a boy nails the boy's eyes to the page
Of the tough algebra he's actually acing at his age.
The average rate of exponential increase: If
X to the zero equals one, Y intercepts. . . It is
The asymptote where the Y functions, equalling why. . .
Down slams Stump's fist. "What?" "Fool, it does not equal Y."
"It does, too." Stump laughs, quivering, his pencil figuring
Beyond the candlelight. Sir Always Right, him, flickering,
Knots of eye whorls and starlessness, Stump, shivering,
Grunts, "Here's the mistake." "What'chya whispering
About?" the fireman asks. "My homework." "Oh."

# *from* Sonnets Broken for America

## Remembrance

Death clanged, hooves iron-shod.
The beast paid witness to the nation's cries to God.
Hooded, with stirrups reversed, the thing trod.
Empty, its saddle.
It trailed the cavalcade.

Kennedy's skull disintegrated into flecks
Of Dallas sunshine. Mercy ran hard, the I-am-
One-with-God rushing like insanity in flicks
Of sirens to save the emergency. No fix.
An open wound.

Death freed a dove,
Wings of white whirling where red and blue flapped above
A many gun salute.

The family filed out of Arlington.
Love left behind a flame,
Eternal.

Blizzards of
Vietnam snowed our dead boys home.
Diamond fluorescence, facets of sky in blue noon,
The hardest jewel, azure, where death knows none,
The light and its crystal dispersion, without name,
A glittering of depths, like fruited plains to reap,
A mirage burned in Arizona's August killing heat.
Air Force tarmac rippled—wings, liquid steel—
A forge fire, a crucible. The pour of molten gold.
Glimmers of conflagrations. Slaves were bought and sold.
Blizzards touched down. They delivered the coffins.

Sacrifice, endless, pulled them from the cargo holds.
Sacrifice, stained with sweat, hauled out the heroes cold.

    Lowered into the dirt's forgetfulness—
Death, too, stirs Hitler's bones.

The funerals erupted,
Napalm.

# The 7th Game of the World Series

## —Following the Pre-game Festivities

At song's end war soars in and roars its rite of screaming
To applause bursting like bombs in air while the brave
Hoot. Stealth shadows shoot swastikas on down through
Hands held heavenward, heil, twilight's red glare gleaming.
What so proudly we hail, death's tech shrieking
Overhead, engines screeching
To cheers so
Gallantly
Seeming
To be the spangled wave
O'er the land of the free and the home of the brave,
The broad stripes and the bright stars. O say, can you see
Proof through the stadium that the flag is still there
When the game bombs? Our pitcher's command?  Lame.
Ball four.

# The Mountaineer

Never to fall,
Never to plummet but with all
The ropes and crampons needed to ascend and defy all
The problems posed by the precipice and the impossible
Summit—To dare and try, to seek and find, but not to yield,
To keep on struggling even when the cumulonimbus world
I look down on, hurls cloud after cloud
On up the rockface—
Lightning makes the mountains twitch
Like crucifixions. Golgotha groans and the lightning's flick
Within each glacial summit valley summons up the infinite
Starveling reject and the bones of forgiveness nailed to reap
A new God out of God. Golgotha thunders. It is God's heartbeat
Stopping. Lightning lights up Christ's sag and earthquakes roll,
Shattering the inner temple.
The Pharisees crucify Jerusalem's
Revolution of the spirit. They reduce festivity to miles of slums
Where guttersnipe and hunger multiply. Doctrine darkens every door.
Billboards paste up propaganda. All are slaves to money's lore.
Dogs peep out, watching the boot stomp and the tread of war.
Hitler rides by like John F. Kennedy. Suffering and desire soar.
Spiritual pollution outdoes the industrial. Even the rich are poor.
Clinical depression reigns. Medication is the nation's overlord.
An addict or a drunk inhabits every tenth door.
The thunderclouds bunch up, taking the mountain cliffs
by storm.

I cannot avoid the approaching storm.
I check my knots and lines.
I pray for a sign
Of change.

# The Great Pacific Garbage Patch

Turning and turning, the widening gyre
In dead, Pacific calm, the center's hold,
Corporate order to enrich the world—
Mere affluence is loosed upon the world.
The trash-dimmed tide is loosed.
The best lack a portfolio, while the worst,
With passionate intensity, invest.

Surely some revelation is at hand.
Surely some great awakening is at hand.
A great awakening! Hardly are those words out
When a vast image out of Spiritus Mundi
Troubles my sight: Up from trash ridden shores,
A shape with maggot body, Hitler's grin,
A gaze blank and pitiless as the sun,
Inches its slow way, while about it
Bacteria grub off the slime
It leaves behind.

A trash whirl, its hour come round at last,
Glacially revolves, ignored, vast,
Somewhere west of California.

## The Indianapolis 500

Engines erupt in mass and scream their crawl
Up tarmac and heat, waved on by the flag
Checkered in promise to make one the brag
Of all our fifty States today.
    Never has such genius given all
To the machine. It foments to destroy the law
Of friction by reversing the wind's lift and drag
While it designs acceleration without lag
In gear, transcending entropy.
  Spirit, pure, burns in claw
And fang. It leaps to the chase and bounds on,
Carnivore in blur, snarl and speed
Hurtling toward the meat,
Victory.
     Brakes
 Screech. Many roll,
Dice. They tumble, batter and explode,
Stars. God, no, not the impact but the blaze
After grabs bones and shakes them free of soul.

## *from* The Ice Storm

## The Ice Storm

*Hour 1, 7 a.m.*

          I stare out at the traffic's epic crawl.
The twelve lanes creep. The treads brake. They slide to a halt.
The car shakes, rumbling. Windows rattle. The doors groan.
Wind and the ice hit like mine machines mangle stone.
The heat, turned to max, battles the freak cold.
I look up at the mirror.
I'm alone.
          Tides touch and swell.
Archangel Aphrodite pearls up from the shell.
Currents of mirrors multiply in many mirrored rays
Multiplying, in turn, in more mirrors where love strays
Out of her birth's upheaval. Into ocean calm she strews
Saffron and platinum, her prism touch, the daybreak's rise.
From far refractions she lifts the near star's white rose.
    Love
Is lore,
Story's seer,
The hidden stirring, the great I
Of visions visioning Earth's radiance, the eye
Made to behold a billion billion suns, which are
Zero parts nothingness if infinite parts star
Without the light pollution, the stars, actual,
Actually seen, celestial
Witnessing.
          Storms bring on the crash
Tornadoing up the shore, the foam's flick, the heave's crush,
The undertow's pull and love's push as sure
As gravity. Out of the surf
She walks,
My wife.
    She,
From the shell, she,
Archangel Aphrodite, foam,

Tidal release, love, her pure form
Unfolds.

*Hour 5, 11 a.m.*

The ice rain won't stop. Gone, the salt. No way to plow.
The iced up traffic blocks me more than four hours now.
Beasts of snow, the cars cram up the twelve lanes and grunt
To grab with hooves and stampede. The herd's affluent.
Whatever of transcendence can be mine is now
Deafened by the roar of the thunder hurling down.
I cut loose a curse as the lightning knifes a wow
In multiples of endlessness. It jags on down,
Cardiograms of heart attacks, suffered now,
A failing ventricle, auricles' oracles, my hurt
Heart. The thunder, a lover's heart-
Beat. Beyond the ice blur and traffic, the old ruse,
Unconditionally unconditional love rules.
            Accidents slide.
      Chain reactions grind their slam.
They slap up body shop fees not covered by love's slim
Insurance plan. I cannot contact my wife.
A widower, a ghostly boo.
I look up at the mirror.  I'm in tears,
A splash of icebergs, Arctic slabs calved free. I fear
Lovelessness, life alone, should my wife be lost,
Like fractals imploding to a point on some list
Reducing life to office politics, love's last
Statistic.
            The stain won't wash off. The assassination's done.
The murder celebrates what cannot be washed clean.
Nature was the king. The pollution is the knife.
The traffic is Macbeth staged in a crime of light.
The twelve lanes, reddened by the back brake lights,
Putter up scarlet, weird exhaust incarnadine,
A witch's gasp, where flecks of ice incarnadine
Oceans of fenders multitudinous.
            I turn to my laptop.

Through my videos I scroll and click on Waikiki
Waves where a heroine takes a tsunami heave,
A surfer champ, her earring, Goth, a fishhook. She
Shoots the curl clean, her pop on down the screen no less
Platinum than seas of a blond dawn here to bless
Oceans with emanations of rebirth and bliss
Mirrored in time's illuminations. Aphrodite's birth
Out of the drowning grip, Waikiki's monster surf—
With superhuman balance, more than the shell, O,
She whooshes like she skis a slope, veers from a shoal
Disaster. She achieves a nine point nine nine nine.
Half of the judges faint. Never has so fine
A try signed lightning, thunderbolts of scrawl,
Her signature flourish, her cursive of no fall,
Love's writing on the wall. Her anklet is a battered
Dolphin, a copper-plated fin and curves of shattered
Grace. There glistens a close-up of her glance from the
Foam. There's her thigh's tattoo, the hieroglyphs of a
Chinese poem meaning, O, God, God knows what.
Reflex and knee jerk, automatic protoplasm,
Brains and a spinal cord, intelligent, the spasm,
What it means to be free, another night's orgasm—
Love's moral temperance defines the man in man.
Mewls of gulls, a wild bay's wings in flight
Where love's more than a sparrow's flit—
To swim there and love each flick
Of wind and light
And wave,
What it means to be free—
            I know why earthquakes heave
Tectonic plates alive. They shift the lava's reach
Up to create new islands. The love goddess seeks.
She finds. Flecked by the foam's touch, she walks clean
Waves. She writes lightning's hieroglyphs up through the sky,
Stroke after stroke, her alphabet spelling out why
Thunder keeps on hammering down such a smash
It makes my ceiling of steel seem to crumple. Ra-
tional or irrational, meaningful or not, cathedral glass

Erupts out of the twelve ice lanes, my childhood school
Where, as a choir boy, I sang ancient songs to soothe
The need for soul, what I've forgotten for so long—
I startle myself, chuckling to remember song
When as a child I belted out hosannas, oh,
Beneath the petals and the azures of a rose
Window. Gethsemane Eastered the dawn sky's
Scarlet slit. First light burned alive the Judas kiss.
Betrayal never should have marred the Jesus wish.
Of the Jew wastrel and His thorn crown sag, "I thirst."
"God, why hast thou forsaken me?" "For they know not
What they do." Nails tear Him as He begs to know why
He writhes in death's agony and can't help His cries
Careening about Golgotha. The skull hill cause
Drops into Hell. And on the third day the heart corpse
Door opens. Dawn folds the shroud, leaves the cave
And walks the road
To Emmaus.
            I
Cannot reach the dodecahedrons I must reach.
The skyline of glass and steel shows off why I, rich
In inner life, know ecstasy, no, not a wretch.
I am sentenced to redeem my lack of sins by
Working myself to death. The soul gags while men drill
For oil in pristine wilderness, promising jobs. Men? Dogs
Witless in desire, prancing up for pets. Love lugs
Herself out of a sewer, offering the devil hugs.
No wonder most go for alcohol and drugs.
Innocence squats. She shoots up.
Drooped, more innocence
Chugs.
The lightning lets loose languages like glossolalia,
A crying of tongues while hands, many, reach for the
Divine.
            Empty
    Wilderness,
Billions of humans, the polluted wilderness, my world—
High school and college wilderness clubs and the wild

Forests and mountains where I forayed alone with
Nothing but a lighter to see how long I could live
Before hunger and too much solitude forced me to give
Up and hike back to roads and cars—Stores where the stench
Of plastic and detergent made me want to wretch.
More than twenty years have gone by and the wilds
Keep emptying out of organisms killed by the
Pesticides by the billions of tons spewed,
Yearly, the many billions spewed.
The wilderness keeps emptying out, like time's on speed,
Like I keep emptying out
Into time.
          The cave
Cathedral opened so far my light found no way
To reach its end of karst pits and hollows, a maze
Of mammals, many millions stirring out of sleep.
I held my light on one. The creature yawned. It blinked.
Wolf-like fangs cut at shadows and the tongue was pink.
The wings stretched out. Claws scratched like they had fleas.
The chitters chased each other's echoes. I walked in like sky
Opened beneath me, a plummet of miles where my light
Illuminated an awakening. Eyelashes and snouts dropped
Like thunderstorms begin. Fur lightninged and I stopped
Where Buddha's eyelid opened, an abyss ledge crack
Crevicing. From it they exploded,
May mountain meltoff,
Currents of whitewater.
          Sounds that would
Haunt me like prayer brought echoes to the wings and were
A temple music, fluttering flits, notes flittering,
Vishnu at his flute, harmonies of scram skittering,
Melodies flickering. The rhythms, hunger gone to flight,
Whether of instinct, mindless, or, intelligent, each flick
And hiss, the rodents surging by
Preserved
Song.
          I could find no reason why
I should not fall in, naturally possessed of soul,

Human, the only animal condemned to buy and sell
To feed.
Into last dusk
Bloodstone and thunderheads of green, I gained
The entrance and looked out at the jungle mountainscape
Where for two hours the bat millions flew from the cave.
They crowded out the evening sky.

The ongoing exponential population explosion causes exponentially exploding environmental ruination. Now even the oceans suffer. Plastic trash pours from the world's rivers or is unceremoniously dumped at high sea. The Great Pacific Garbage Patch is only the most mammoth of the ocean's many plastic trash gyres. It is the size of a small continent and nothing stops its ever enlarging. When washed, the billions of tons of petroleum-based synthetic clothes leach nanoplastics. These chemicals drain off with the world's washing machine wastewater, joining the rivers running down into the seas. Soon the ocean's mass of plastic will outweigh that of its fish. Organisms go extinct daily and the significance of this loss is not publicly discussed. We are in the midst of a sixth mass extinction. A new era is dawning, the Anthrocene, in which human being predominate. Those marred by nugatory aesthetic sensitivity feel no despair at this loss of the living things around us.

Industrialism's power structure, dependent on quarterly stock and bond returns, proves incapable of stopping the pollution. Nationalists everywhere play the totalitarian propaganda game, denying global warming's existence or poohpoohing its significance because the changes needed to stop global warming would compromise their power and wealth. At best the nationalists throw up their hands and declare nothing can be done. What is needed to stop the world's coasts from being flooded out is the conversion of Earth's coal power plants to zero emissions coal power plants thirty years ago. But it was not done and will not be done because such reform would hit the economy. Of course every three months a business must perform or its shares lose value. Of course this fact forces short term actions which are, of course, long term destructive. Ditto the election system. True and substantial pollution reform would hurt jobs in the short term and whatever party is in power would be voted out, the reforms reversed by the incoming party.

Perhaps nature's perishing necessitates a revolution in mass consciousness. Such radical transformation occurred during the Second Great Awakening, but the resulting anti-slavery movement upset the vested interests to such an extent the Civil War resulted, our most bloody historical event. Such a revolution in consciousness would probably be led by an avatar, but the examples of Martin Luther King and Mahatma Gandhi prove instructive. Both suffered assassination. Prophetic compassion and self-sacrifice exist, as embodied by personages such as Jesus of Nazareth and Shakyamuni, but the modern secularization, the widespread lack of belief, is not a coincidence. All religions warn against the cultivation of desire, but the desire for consumer goods and the economics of the buying and selling of such goods, provide the basis of our so-called affluence. A soul besotted by desire is not capable of religious experience.

Nature is dying.

*Hour 7, 1 p.m.*

There's how my wife agreed to wed.
I proposed where a sushi bar's gold leaf and pearl screen bled
Mirroring reeds and clean water. There loomed two red
Crowned cranes, them mated for life, Japan's emblem of the blood
And immortality of marriage. O, God, my God, my love bit a bit
Of scallops raw, cleared her throat, let her chopsticks fall
To her plate. "Uhmmm... Huh..." "I care about you." "That's all?"
I dared pull out the ring. "Forever, I—" "Yes. No."
"No? You—" "This is forever, I. Not no. Yes." "O."
We sipped sake brewed from a temple's snow,
April's cold beginnings, a stroll into gates
Where love begets
Erratics
Curling off the tongue, her choice, the very best
Sake in the joint, three little bottles downed to wrest

Harmony from our love negotiations cooed to test
For the ways she and I could live together lest
We failed to live at all. To live at times, at least.
Scallops on the half shell, like a gift from above,
Appeared upon the table. Aphrodite rippled, of
Seaward's shucked open, of the fluids, currents of—
Newly engaged, we stared at the shellfish glistening,
The roar of some inner, some hidden whispering—
The pull of currents when the shell becomes the sea—
That date when the love goddess made my love agree
To marry.

*Hour 9, 3 p.m.*

Stormcaught for nine hours now,
I wonder why we have to die the way we do.
The respirators keep on wheezing to prolong
Whatever brain reactions happen when a lung
Mechanically expands and contracts, while a line
Rises like Himalayan summits, a cardiograph
Registering last life and a downbeat's halt, relief,
Dead even. The code blue event makes doctors save
A soul time after time after time. Ethics, yes, are grave.
Death, desecrated, desecrates us all. Like when my mom
Died of bone cancer. She gaped, alive in death's womb,
Clouded by tubes like veins—placental, her last room—
Transfusions to the fetus, birth shrunk in pain's womb—
Caesarian in her need for knives to cut the doom
Out. She believed death a gift. She knew Paradise
Would open, taking her. She died, entering Paradise.
At least that's what I saw. Her soul rose into light.
Rays opened and absorbed her. A white rose light,
Love's wings pure and an angel's embrace took to flight.
In radiance the vision carried my mom into Paradise.
God knows hallucinations cannot be confirmed by faith.
God knows what humans really need. Perhaps it's faith.
For weeks Mom huddled, rasping, but she did not die.
She grimaced out of the remains of her face, which cried,

"It's time for me to speak to you." "You're okay?" "Why,
No, I'm not dead yet. My son, listen when I speak to you.
There are some hard truths about me. I cannot tell—"
"Mother—" "A just God would drop me into Hell."
She stared up like a predator. "But, about you.
Times are when I think I know too much about you.
Your life has not been good to you. I see how you've—"
She paused while a nurse took the chart and left a scrawl
Like lightning blipped out of a plug ripped from the wall.
"Do you deny the truth of what I say?" I managed, "Mom—"
"Whatever it is, stop. Have the strength to." "What? Mom—"
"An empty promise to the dead's a curse." "But, I love you."
"Is that all you have to say to me? 'I love you?'" "Well, I do."
There was no more to say. Of course, that was not coarse.
Mom stared at me as nature took its course.
She made not a sound. Her soul rose.
A light gave way to endless ends.
She dissolved into them.

*Hour 10, 4 p.m.*

Blizzard blare
Blasts, whiteout blear,
Claws and hunger, a cougar's leap and blur.
The snarl and the swipe, blinding fangs, the ice storm's pure
Necessity. The thighs spring and the throat growls out its wail.
Too many guts, too much digestion, the snow is a whirl
Obscuring wilderness where trucks and icebound cars,
Most idling, lend heat to those within. There is a cause.
It's final but few will ever own up to it. No one cares.
The animal lunges. It hurls from the storm.
The victim, raked. Hit again, hurls like stone
April runoff tears away. The wounds can leave no stain.
The bite to the throat, the crunch and the rip, do more than stun.
I fear for my soul. I am afraid to dare get out there and implore.
I cannot get out and beg them to get back into their cars. More
And more are abandoning their cars. They are entering pearl blur.
They are blind in snow so thick shadows fail and only the shapes of

Dark objects can be discerned, love
Reduced to objects, dark, the whited out.
The blizzards makes of them little more than fairytale,
A winter without end, as if there's nothing left to tell
But bedtime stories lulling us to sleep in April snow.
As if my soul's awakening. But there's nowhere to go.
Fear of death chains me. I, a prison coward. No,
My wife might be perishing. One among many dead.
Too many are already dead. The cellphones, dead.
Even the internet, gone. My wife's stumbled into snow.
Like murder's mangled her, she sprawls in springtime snow.
I find and heave her body out like bridegrooms lift
Brides across thresholds of suites opening aloft
Galaxies but she's dead.
                Crystalline,
        The diamond structure, a
Metastable equilibrium, kinetic, bonds to share,
Octahedron crystals, the unbreakable here to assure
The facets' architecture and its sheer
Shuddering in the
Hand
Is
Beauty
But I do not know if she is dead.

Extreme hypothermia triggers vasoconstriction. The blood retracts, keeping the inner organs warm. The skin, bloodless, whitens and the victim, now a snowman, pays witness to the absolute, perhaps. He hallucinates. Whether of loved ones or of the soul's white rose oneness with what is called God, the nature of these visions remains subject to no empirical confirmation.

The victim tears off his clothes. Called paradoxical undressing, this phenomenon, too, remains unexplained. Theorists hypothesize that the skin's blood vessels suddenly dilate. An unbearable rush of heat like lava causes the undressing.

The victim burrows. One can readily surmise that freezing to death triggers the primitive part of the brain, the brain stem. Survival instincts trigger the burrowing.

Death follows quickly.

*Hour 11, 5 p.m.*

Probably, my wife's at home
Bent over her desk, laboring to the hum
And tick of our grandfather clock, each tock like cliffs
Crumble and create an avalanche. God, the tears slide
Like mountains down my face, the collapse slowed
To a drip by the valley ridge and ravine lines
Glaciers gouged out, my ice
Age.

Man, keep calm.
She's probably okay. She's probably at home.
Go ask the dinosaurs. Mounted bones gape. They roar,
"The odds? Nil. Probability ruled out the meteor.
When the four mile wide stone chunk pierced the atmosphere—
Lucifer tumbling out of Heaven, his scream and wings on fire—
We animals were only doing what we had to do.
We looked up, grunting as death tore apart the sky.
Nothing but luck. The impact emitted such a wave
Of heat Earth went apocalyptic and the flames
Killed ninety nine point nine nine nine percent of life,
Leaving Man to descend from rodents, which survived."
Probably,
My wife's okay.

Probability cannot answer why the lightning is.
Probability goes berserk as the bolt zeroes in.
Only love answers why the victim takes the hit.
Love's lightning litters the land like good luck.
How love electrifies strikes me as no reason to duck.
What lightning lets me behold leaves me thunderstruck.

*Hour 13, 7 p.m.*
Gone, the storm.
Last light delivers calm.
Radiance twists and the sky's designs
Web alive daylight's rupture. Nighttime climbs
From the anchor point to the capture spiral, clasps
The frames spun and the radii, arachnid tasks,
An egg sac guarded by eight eyes, last dusk
Hunched over the remains of day,
Another dark
Beginning.

The gloam
Is molybdenum
Strengthening steel. In iron ore,
Manganese. Yttrium to crystallize the alloy's core.
Amalgams of selenium, molecular process, inner lore,
Austentic chromium, the iron allotrope,
Iron's other form,
No trap.

An opal,
Harlequin.

A play.

Art's laughter.

*Hour 14, 8 p.m.*
My love and I
Rented out a chapel laced
With Tiffany, glass of a pink lake interlaced
With blossoms of mauve, reeds magenta traced.
Kingfishers flamed like fireworks, haloing her face
Wreathed in a lapis lazuli leaf. Her lips, azure toned—
Crowned chalcedony, rays in chrysolite, she posed.
Tiffany copied from life. Her brow, bold, big boned.

She looked uncomfortable, seated on her throne.
Her robes of beryl,
Ravines of
April runoff.
Beauty's peace,
Above the altar reigned this Jazz Age masterpiece.
The June noon blue sky turned it chrysoprase.
The silk she ordered from Japan: Chrysoprase.
She herself made the bridal gown. Chrysoprase,
Even the threads she used to stitch it. Chrysoprase,
She marched up the aisle. She stepped up.
She frowned.
Veiled.
Face to face.

Architectures of shattered glass, my marriage lost,
The superstructure's form and balance, rust
Crumbling away, the junkyard lots
Death, like a jester, dices for,
My city torn,
A waste.
I'm caught where toss
After toss tumbles up snake eyes—
The math cannot be right—
Calculus of the finite, tangents figured to a sine,
The complex of identities broken, some sum,
Differentials differentiating this lust from that lust
When the difference is the all of it, at least
Some derivation from the mean, no, not a list
Reducing love to office politics.
A convergence though the dread
Equations cannot be solved
Analytically—

*Hour 15, 9 p.m.*
Bullhorns.
Troop carriers. The army's here.

A searchlight blinds me. It blinks away, leaving tracks
Like neon blipping ads, my retinae trashed
By helicopter searchlights. Beam
After beam burns
Like ash
On fire.
Salvation speaks of the curse, time.
The tragedy resounds in stone, an April tomb. The snow
Hit like the freak storms meteorologists have long foretold.
Too late to dismiss death like it is a fearmonger's doom.
Too many have perished already. Helicopters loom.
The blades hover like my delusions. They near and lash
Up the snow. The mess smears my windshield like the glass
Crumbles and plummets into bitty flits of wings and ash
Transfigured into a glimpse of a straw-bound ache
Whose crèche and newborn, candlelit, will always ache
For those in need.
            Blood of the lamb
Coursed through an angel's arteries and, limb by limb,
Lent radiance and craft to a madwoman's hand.
Like Sartre being honest, she walked through a traffic jam.
She gestured, blessing, calling out, "Handmade, a crèche.
Five dollars for a handmade crèche." The traffic crept.
I gave her fifty-five. "Why, sir! God bless you, sir.
I'll pray for you."
"Thank you."
            Whittled out of plywood, a scrap's blur,
Animals worked from refuse, here reigns the child
No bigger than a fingernail. The manger's dim
Cradling in firelight and straw, all the dun
Mules stabled near the corner's sty—
Every cold breath, a mist of ice,
Turns at the approach of the three
Wise.
            Above the wilderness, an angel cries,
"Fear not. I bring you tidings of great joy."

*Hour 18, Past Midnight*
Earliest a.m. eyes rapid, movement of
Retinae firing alive mammal brains to dove
Alive dead Aphrodite, twitching hard, I dream
Juliet sprawls, drugged, lit up by her tomb
Torchlight. Night dew soaks her and her slab
In columns porphyry and the marble tiles her dad
Festooned with lilies pale to honor his child dead.
Robes of gold filigree enshroud her like she is dead.
Romeo crowbars his way in. Stones can warm to love's touch.
Romeo touches stone, groping in. He holds up a torch.
Its flickering flares hard, shadowing Juliet's truth.
Romeo intones, "In death we will plight our troth."
Juliet stirs with all the knowing of an April seed,
A gathering in warmth, germinations roused to leaf,
Lingering in long life. Her eyelids flick. They lift.
She has begun to see. Her pupils twitch. Idiot
Romeo opens poison like teen love, turned suicide,
Cleanses the suffering, purifying love's tomb time.
"In death we're one." Juliet shudders. Her head shakes.
Romeo curses his imaginings. "My love awakes.
She's dead. Death, not she—O, my God, she wakes."
Juliet stretches, yawns hard. She sits up. She blinks.
At her shroud she cries, "Mama's dressed me up in chintz.
It figures. Mother always did love kitschy crap like this.
I'm changing." "Juliet, you're alive. Do I wake
Or sleep?" "Get with it. You're awake."
Suicide, ice, dissolves.
They escape,
Married,
Free.

I dream
I'm Aphrodite's groom
Carrying my bride away from ice-
Choked exits and the downtown tower skies
Bleared by totalitarian design, where death
Thrives. "There must be an answer to this dearth,"

I proclaim, carrying my love up to the earth
Sweeter than white rose afterlives, Montana dirt
Where Maytime mountains change the light like love
Shadows change on the wall. Slopes redden and the dusk
Unclothes the nighttime's nakedness. Tonight, the dark
Can't happen fast enough.

I dream
Only a fool calls the labor sweet.
Too many times a minute bees wings have to beat,
Eleven thousand four hundred times. The bugs seek
To find among the waste lots and the tumbleweeds.
For all the insecticide and the human weeds, wings seek
Out their crowds of hive brethren, bringing nectar news.
They choreograph maps and on out the workers cruise.
Per tablespoon, it's twenty thousand odysseys too rife
With death when forty-two days are all they have of life.
It takes one hundred thirty-five thousand miles of flight—
That's five and a half times around Earth—to get but a pint
Of honey. God knows what possibly could be the point
Unless the taste, in itself, keeps us from the pit.
The bees roar, taking flight.

I dream
The great beekeeper, Aphrodite, takes her share.
Being's bee whisperer, she takes all, takes no care,
Dons not a helmet or mask screen to stop the stings.
Hives she cuts open. Attack after attack clings
To her, a bee coat. By the billions, not one stings.
She rips another hive open. Out the wings soar.
Her whispering calms the lightning and sting storm.
Bees quiet after harvest takes their lifeblood's store.
They quiet beyond silence, murmuring, a frail fire,
Canticles devoid of fuel, songs robbed of their life.
As if love's work delivers them the death they need,
The harvesting scraps away their survival's feed.
They perish, having pollinated April's seed.

I dream
Love sprawls, refrigerated in a morgue. She
Spreads like dawn on her slab, a morning prism
Caused by ice clouds' hexagonal crystals, schisms
Of polar daylight fracturing to unfold another sum
Derived from farthest north's illuminations, some
Solution posed by the refractions, a star split in three,
Mock sun phenomena, illusions born of the total freeze,
The triple sun beheld above the Arctic Circle. The stars three
Bring on love visions as I trek down Alaskan shores to seek
And find where glaciers calve off and
Float away. It is a world-destroying flood
Mirroring the trio radiance, a dawn of love
Found below a morgue light bulb, love
Examined in an official inquisition of
Who's
Who in rigor mortis. Her chart reads,
"Here lies John's doe," as if all she needs
Is a positive identity.

I dream the Milky Way,
Aphrodite's halo, love's crown born
Of nebulae, the dust cloud orbit, the star foam
Within coalescing matter and heat, where planets form
In gravity and time, where new life goes on being born
Like the determinations have a mind,
Nestling, as one,
Aphrodite's
Two,
Like spoons they fit as one, asleep. The streetlights pry
In through the edges of the shades. The shadows, light,
Frolic as wind stirs the courtyard trees.

I dream.
Well into her ninth month, Aphrodite
Walks the ice road. She should not be there, but she's there.
A car careens by, honking like she's nothing but a deer,
Hits her, speeds away. Like no one could really care,

She and her belly slide, slamming up a side rail.
Her spine and skull smash, a twist's sprawl,
Her mouth agape and leaking
Industrial effluents,
Azures of
Antifreeze,
Sludge sliming harbors,
Fertilizer killing estuaries and another river delta dead,
Shorelines dead for the children to explore.

My eyelids open.
My retinae take in an exit red,
Flames out of a sign signifying the Hell dead.
Almost awakening, I shout, "Prison. In Hell.
Hell is the lack of beauty. It makes me unfree.
The world stripped of its beauty incarcerates me."
My eyes drip oceans, the forgotten, the polluted seas,
Islands of affluence, oceans of poverty and dread,
Shores of petroleum, currents of mercury and lead.
An oil rig explodes. Estuaries fill with billions dead.
Gills drop from the crude. Fish flop. They crowd shores.
Oil-slicked birds gape like they have been to war.
Blowsy and meadowish, maggots gorge.
Oil-soaked
Dead,
Shores of America, the beautiful—

I wake.
In scarlet looms a clock's
Quarter after midnight. The one through twelve mocks
All attempts at irrationality. The order of it tocks
Its tick like logic works love's cause. Reddening makes
The exit clear. The exit sign denotes the spirit's mix
Of clarity and despair. I am lucky, I admit.
The Marines rescued me. Like from a casket's care,
Soldiers grabbed and pulled me up out of my car.
The armored carrier I boarded—others made me room.
Drove past the wreckage and death caused by the ice storm.

Fed a cheese sandwich. Shown where I could sleep.
A Red Cross shelter, a ramshackle public school.
Our children subject to—The nation is a fool.
Blankets were to be had, but they were not enough
For all the citizens thronging the old gymnasium.
The blankets ran out after me. To a girl and
Her baby I gave mine away. Like dumping sand,
Onto her arm I draped it. Hurried hard away.
"Thank you, sir." I said nothing. Went away.
Led by a volunteer, took shelter in a
Room with many like myself.
"Sleep here."
"All right."

What I call my soul falls
Like Antarctica's ice shelf slides down fells
Bouldering down to Hell's
Ice
Lake.
I plummet
Into the ice abyss, bottomless-
Ness mirroring me like a frozen wishing well.
At my reflections I stare, tumbling into deepest Hell.

In Red Cross shelter, I dream I
Quit. Graduate. School. Drove. Nine. Days. Alone
Until I found a trail and winter camped. Alone,
I bent by my fire, staring at its maze to know
Why I should go on floundering. The drifts of snow
I struggled through brought hypothermia and sleep.
I risked death, camped on a mountain slope.
I did not care how often I would slip.
For all the ages I'd spent studying, my dream
Of publication. No. It had all become a scream.
No, I could not. Could not complete my PhD.
All about Romeo and Juliet. On Shakespeare. Gee.
Drove alone for nine days, without sleep, no dream,
The ever darkening, the sunlight perishing, a scream

Echoing ever further out West. But to die, a blear
Of dusks and motels, cheap beds and a cheaper blur
Lighting up an old Gideon—Bent in prayer, sure—
In Glacier National Park I found a way to die
By hiking into snow, wind-sculpted,
Wind-torn
Drifts,
The promise of the forms,
The architecture of the snow,
The frolic architecture of the snow,
Announced by all the trumpets of the sky
Where swan-like forms invest a hidden thorn
Witnessed in a Montana mountainside of storm,
Not arrays of abstractions, but, the snowy forms,
Entrances beyond the plowed parking lots, the forms
Like arches leading to an architecture, white rose sky.
I broke away from the trails, blazed on into white rose sky.
My ice cleats gripped like claws. My ice pick hooked the sky.
I pulled my body up.
Ceaseless sweat. Wind. No, I would not turn back.
No matter how the sky kept opening, I would not turn back.
I topped a cliff.
There loomed a cougar.
From summits the fur and fangs leapt.
Grace gravely granted, the thing landed, and it crept
Like snow begins to avalanche. It prowled out of a depth
Of drifts in twigs stunted and mountain waste. Like death
Echoes out of its own resounding, the thing growled.
I did not believe in it. The hallucination inched
So close I could have petted it. When it talked, I flinched.
"You think I am an angel?" it said, "Like I'm from the sky?
Don't. I am dirt and blood and murder. You,
Even you laugh inside to know I claw and toy
Entrails from my meat alive, a dog held down by my
Claws. I make the dog beg to die. It whines to die.
But you are not a dog.
Stop whining.
Your heart beats not for death."

I mountaineered beyond the sky,
Struggling up to white rose realms of why
Each hammer slam and rope up clung to summit ice
So opaline it spoke of afterlives and why, O, why
Beauty beyond pure beauty revealed boulder heights
To conquer though it was all blizzards and cirque ice.
I paused to behold it all, a cliff drop near
Forty miles, a fall into sheer
Ice
Arctic
Emptiness,
Plains of tundra trailing far beyond the mountain ranges
In ruination and the warming bringing on death's changes.
I'd given up. Nature's dead. It is hopeless. It deranges.
Clearly delusional, I know I had become a ghost,
A haunting haunted by myself, myself alone,
Northernmost, no, not human, not more fear of falling,
Not bound by ropes and the crampons to keep from fouling
The crags below, no, not more hammering in to keep from failing,
Plummeting, no, but hunger desiccated, eye pits in search,
Bones in subzero wind, a cliffside perch,
Talons spectral, wings like rags,
An extinct bird of prey.

I dropped.
I leaned down into my wings' spread and reach.

I caught the wind's lift.

I dream.
In Aphrodite's womb,
Escaping the condition of a worm,
Cells multiply, nuclei by the many trillions all
Mitosis and the differentiations ruled by laws
Of ribosomes and DNA, the code, organic cause,

The folds on folds placental, rhythms diastole,
Cycles of pressure, systole, auricles of oracle,
Valve and aortal prophesies, a newfound pulse
When April's snowmelt quickens and the runoff's pace
Thunders out of the foam and boulders, the stream's wild
Turmoil. The face contracts, become a smile
Or frown of pain. The suffering is not animal.
The embryo evolves beyond the stages animal.
From fish to bird to the mammalian stare
Braced to take on a human's share
Of grace,
Grace
To be this child,
Grace
To be this boon—
The child stirs, struggling to be born.

        I dream
    Juliet sprawls, slabbed
Among agate-encrusted columns. Her blood's slowed,
Tomb noise noiseless, clockless quiet, a pulse slurred
To mumbling by magic mimicking death's Arctic cold.
        Cocooned,
Of all things butterfly, love creates her own chrysalis
Chrysoprase birthing free. She monarchs up a flick
On off to Paradise.
        She warms the family tomb.
The lack light obscures her curled in death's womb.
New lives of tissues cradle her like snow turns warm
On April afternoons. She stirs, beginning to be born.
Romeo's approach shadows the rot and torch gloom.
He weeps like his love's lowered into Hell flames torn
By what all desire but none can have. His brains? Gone.
Somehow the fool believes death cannot be rewritten.
The need to end his life has left the poor man smitten
By poetry. He recites a poem about a thorn bitten
Off a rose. Juliet chortles. She opens her eyes. She sits up.
Romeo stops with all the poetry. He ponders love

And irreality. "Delusions," he says, "Blast to break
My brains like hydrogen bombs mushroom up to shake
Whole continents apart." Juliet laughs like it's a joke.
"Juliet?" "My love?" "Speak true. Do I wake
Or sleep?" "We got away with it.
We are free.
Let's flee."

Aesthetic experience, the transcendence of suffering through pleasure, is as inevitable a bodily process as the liver facilitating lipid metabolism or the left ventricle's contractions thrusting oxygenated blood into the aorta. Even the vaunted phrase, "the meaning of life," pays tribute to the aesthetic. That no meaning in life can actually be experienced means that the existent cannot accept what aesthetic or, sensory stimulation, experience offers him. He is deprived of an essential bodily need, the ecstasy provided by contact with the beautiful. He falls into depression or some other form of mental illness, usually common neurosis, where the self cannot accept the conditions in which it is forced to live. Sensations of imprisonment and rage assault. The existent spirals down into an abyss of an ever-deepening negativity.

Religion has and can satisfy aesthetic needs. The ongoing litany of feasts and ceremonies offered by the Medieval Christian calendar, as well as the variety provided by the changes of the seasons and the shifting agricultural cycle, brought relief to the suffering self. Variety is the spice of life. Variety is the basis of positive aesthetic experience. It provides different—i.e. new and refreshing—sensory stimulation. How much drudgery we must endure in our ever-repeating jobs causes much of our suffering. But religion has the advantage of providing the inner life with unity, of oneness with the divine or whatever we wish to call it. Unity is also the basis of all aesthetics. Contemplating a great painting vaults us into a unity of self and perception. What the senses provide becomes realized by the consciousness. Beauty is perceived. Here is why aesthetics and religion have always been allied. Music, sculpture, painting, architecture—art—overwhelm in abundance with a visit to any cathedral. Art provides the oneness, the unity, which is both the beautiful and the divine.

Here the story of the contemporary American tragedy unfolds. Failed industrialization, while spoiling nature and forcing its citizens into ever-repeating, aesthetically dull jobs, does not spread affluence. The vast majority are poor. The industrialization, while providing good food, clothing and shelter, also pollutes and forces the nine to five deprivations. Not provided are industrialism's benefits, such as generally available and—thriving—educational and cultural institutions. Few but the elites gain, creating a kind of plantation economy, where most do not prosper, where slavery and serfdom, though called something else, actually abound. Such failure has long maligned what has been called the Third World. Now this failure mars the United States. Natural resources, depleted both by pollution and population explosion, result in too much scarcity and once affluent individuals find themselves marginalized and impoverished.

Many turn to the consolations of demagoguery. Donald Trump's election was no fluke, but an inevitable aspect of an economy which is now ever more failing to provide. President Trump masterfully appealed to the formerly affluent, who are chronically neurotic. Their desires and what their society allows them are so at odds that they, deeply wounded, descend into the infernal and take delight in thuggery, warmongering and God knows what else. Witness the infamous Nazi Nuremburg rallies. Google up videos of the yearly extravaganza. See aesthetic oneness provided in spades. Of course, Germany, impoverished by WWI's aftermath, had been an affluent society. Its experience is not unique. From its status as one of the wealthiest countries, from the 1930s military takeovers, misguided economic policies and other tragic events destroyed Argentina. In the 1970s, the nation descended. Its government abducted, tortured and killed some tens of thousands of its own citizens.

Without quality aesthetic experience, a society's moral rigor atrophies and a cancer of hatred and murderousness metastasizes.

*Hour 20, 2 a.m.*
I dream time's hoax
Disintegrates, Kyoto's husk,
Harvests done, skies of winnowing and chaff cloud dusk
Time tears away. The empty fields kill hunger and the dark,
Nightmare gods. There looms Buddha's weather-beaten blur,
A statue in reeds and pines, by a pondside late light blear,
Emerald eruptions far from crowds and the subway's blare.
I am done with the ruination. Here the cherry petals reign.
A gust takes them and they float and settle on down away
Where regicide and the screams of true dynastic change
Drift down to a famed garden path. The blossom reign
Hurls deluge, lightning hieroglyphs, time's thunder rune
Scattered in sevens and fives, tanka of the done,
Calligraphy's brushwork flicked like what is done
Is always song. The blossoms keep on raining down.
They're never done. The inn door reveals weeds,
Jumbles of dirt and crannies, like death breathes
Alive an entranceway. Beckoning gapes. It's a
Collapse, a shambles given many stars by the
Most reputable guidebook. I have no-
Where else to go.
Blossoms keep cascading off a rim,
A lantern lit, a post of living cedar and a rhyme
Of lilies by the *ryokan* door.

I dream a *shoji* door, within, slides back.
In walks a spirit, a *kitsune,* a white fox, Noh-masked,
A stare of chipped paint and fangs. Ancient, her growl's rasp,
Wind in a newfound temple pool, like papers rip,
A rustling and surge when time at last has turned ripe
For laughter. The fox perks her ears. There's winter's rap
At the door, an unbidden guest, the touch of snow
Within the pine and cherry twigs, fresh fallen snow,
A clinging not yet melting away, April snow,
Rare, a delight. The fox takes off her mask, shapeshifts,
Become a crone in rags, a toothless hunch, time's myth.
The inn's proprietress, she sets out a tray with
Sake fit for an emperor.

I dream
A roof of straw thatch thick like prayer, a house
Of no nails, no, not one, like iron were too hard
A presence—Gables of cypress made to uphold
Presence. It is home of the goddess of the sun,
Amaterasu, the light beckoning to those undone
By life and loss. Divine regalia, hidden, adorn
An inner room, a within long forbidden to behold,
Where only the emperor ventures. He takes hold
Of a holiest mirror, polished bronze,
Hexagonal tin and brass
Reflections of
Amaterasu,
Purity.

I dream.
On my plane trip from Kyoto, I have a window seat.
Beyond the jet's wing, the Aleutian Islands dawn,
This April's Arctic archipelago, caught in its time,
Mountainous, all slopes and summit spines of ice.
They take in the light like there is no end to light
No matter what. From Earth's diurnal turn,
Filtering from its rise, the sun
Heaves into sight,
A wedge
Burning out of its own scarlets.

I dream
Kyoto crooked paths,
Storefronts of pottery, tea bowls to buy and clasp,
To sip and ponder conflagrations within the kiln ash,
Burnt into the glaze, bone imprints borne by the flames
And the marrow disintegrations, the skull change
Fired to a glow while branches, left within the kiln,
Becoming ash, rip at the glaze like time can kill
Beauty, bowls become beauty of the
Torn and the
Ugly.

Many bowls crack. The faults slip. Firestorms rage.
Continents of earthquakes plummet. Flames unleash
Whirlwinds of heat. The cyclones typhoon in and lash
The half-baked and the badly formed. The misplaced crash
To the kiln floor. They fling up dust and soot like trash
Invades the workings whirling within.

*Hour 21, 3 a.m.*
            The exit sign
  Brightens to visibility a path,
A straight and narrow passageway. The guiding light
Like God lets silence gain a voice, a Christ-like sigh
Whispering of Golgotha. It tells why sacrifice
Sagged, the fly-ridden crown, the thorns and twitch
Nailed on display, death spasms and a soul's lightning flick
Down into underworlds where the forgotten rove and flit.
He sought to heal the broken, the blind and the maimed.
There looms the exit, red. It spells out a way of escape
Should fire or ice bring on the soul's old soulful date,
A glow, scarlet, in Red Cross shelter here to keep
A room dark for the living who, like me, need sleep.
            But I can't sleep,
Wondering why my mother hurt, a ghost of tin
Clattering on the stairs, a specter rattling torn
Pieces of herself, the scrape and clash of a tune
Like car accidents, a bash screeching and a stunned
Look like some inner moral battle, some last stand,
Fights on when it is all over. I never understood.
Mom bent in prayer. She haunted her cathedral stained
By forms of God in gemmed glass where I sat in wait.
Mom sought pastoral counseling while I had to wait.
My favorite window shone in amber where the word
Appeared on the road to Emmaus, wild
Paths,
Harvest wheat.
His robes, grain and the ripening of an April world.

One window eked the light
Of phosphorescence, fueled by phosphorus,
The luminescence without visible energy source,
The lantern's radiance. It was held up by Christ.
Oxidation, slowly burning phosphorus—
The more dark, the more light
The lamp emitted.

*Hour 22, 4 a.m.*
Like stirring out of death,
Part of me wakens, witnessing love's stray
Unwanted soul, a reject, Magdalene. On Easter day,
With angels having pushed the rebirth's cave stone door away,
The reject brings water and a basket full of myrrh and frankincense
To cleanse Christ's corpse. She enters, having to clean up God's death.
She gropes, not knowing why she touches nothing but the death
of death.
She kneels and seeks and finds the cave floor strewn with
nothing less
Than the face napkin neatly folded and the shroud
Cast off, an outer layer shed,
A husk, and what should
Be, released,
The seed,
Gone.
Magdalene hurries away to tell how death cries joy and proof aloud.

REM flash
Cardiographs a blip, a vital sign
Signaling the flat truth, the heart's end. Every time,
As love defibrillates the corpse, hearts jump like rhyme,
Proving there's life yet in a cardiograph's dead even line.
It brings blood torrents to the heart, May's deluge song,
Thunder, the mountains' snowmelt roaring on and on,
Cascades and boulders, bashed, like what has been
Never was, like the ice and snow have never been.
"Don't you dare let them drug me anymore. My son,

If I am to die, I want to see how this dying's done."

My eyes
Mississippi. They delta such a flood
They leave the lowlands and all the States a blur of
Mom
And God.

*Hour 24, 6 a.m.*
First
Light's
Chalcopyrite,
Chrysoberyl,
Aventurine,
Fluorspar,
Tourmaline
In twigs of ice. To see
Why beauty cries aloud along the streets,
I sidle on up to the shelter's windowpanes,
Rust-flaked, institutional green paint,
A public school, ramshackle
Fenestration.

First
Light's
Peridot,
Jacinth,
Malachite,
Hornblende,
A cat's eye
In twigs of iolite
And pearl.

First
Light's
Holosiderite,
Cupronickel,

Argentite,
Nichrome,
Zirconium,
Electrum
In throes of conflagrations, a child playing with fire.
He ignites paper towels. The flick and flurry of the flames march on,
Puppets parading in pink buttons and the silver-plated bling
Called just another day, hexagonal symmetry,
Near tetrahedral bonding angles,
Ice.

First
Light's
Olivine,
Heliotrope,
Carnelian,
Elinvar,
Dolomite.

First
Light's
Chrysolite,
Adamant,
Obsidian,
Aquamarine,
In ice.

*Hour 25, 7 a.m.*
Whatever for,
Risen, the sun's there. It has a core
Pressurized to 26.5 petapascals, letting fusion's proton-proton chain
Occur each second 930,000,000,000,000,000,000,000,000,000,
000,000,000
Times, relentless churn,
The burn,
27 million degrees Fahrenheit.

Whatever for,
The radiation zone transits via angular shear,
Stratified turbulence, the solar plasma's instability
Arising from non-axisymmetric field components,
The tachocline, which hurls in differential rotation,
Driving the solar dynamo.

Whatever for,
Helioseismology and the need for sun lore
Use eigenfunctions as well as spectral emission lines
To examine monotonic decreases in angular velocity,
Torsional eruptions, adiabatic perturbations,
Resonant modes of oscillation,
A ceaseless, chaotic
Nimbus.

Whatever for,
The heliosphere passes beyond the planets and the Kuiper Belt and
the Oort Cloud
Until it fades, become one with the interstellar radiation,
Having reached its end,
The termination zone.

Whether beyond the termination zone
The sun's irradiation exists at all, is a matter of
Speculation.

For billions of years the sun will burn in a state of quiescent
equilibrium.

Like a child I perch on the shelter's windowsill.
I'm in the now, forgetting that what happens will
Happen. I'm gazing at the early morning sun,
Fusion's irradiance low on the ice skyline
No longer scarlet, risen, a refraction's long

Mirroring inward and a multiplicity within
Mind working true to love's myriad phases
Like looking at a mirror reveals many faces
In a face, my own face betraying traces
Of laughter and none of the challenges of the
Struggle to live a moral life, like there is a
Moral center.
I
Recall the shrine to Amaterasu,
Japan's goddess of the sun. As if to woo
Radiance, I prayed for the light to spare my soul
The malaise, the miasma, anomie caused by the prose,
The routine, a dull life, blood without the white rose
Paradise.
My wife and I
Walked the shrine's trails. We found a stream,
Like shattered mirror glass, clean water, the light strewn
By gravity's pull and the foam's blur where a monstrous carp
Took to the current, helping itself ease and struggle up
The stream. The backflow and push of the vacuum's surge
Created by the giant body's leeside helped it creep
Upstream. A backbone and a spread of nerves
Fired its fluids alive, a brain and an urge
To gain against the stream.

# SELECTED POEMS

# *from* Jinzhou 1985 Northeast China

*In 1985, my wife and I took teaching positions at a college in Liaoning Province, Jinzhou City, northeast China. The first Westerners to live there since the Chinese Revolution of 1949, we had some adjustments to make. A society hobbled by debilitating poverty, along with a people recovering from the chaos and violence brought on by the Cultural Revolution, made for a difficult experience. Communist propaganda regarding the moral qualities of citizens of the United States did not help.*

*My wife and I will forever be in debt to Mr. Mu Zhang Ying, the head of the English department. He essentially took us into his family. His warmth, his humor, as well as his explanations, allowed us to cope with misunderstandings we experienced. Due to Mr. Mu, we were able to stay for three years, gaining invaluable knowledge and experience. The details of the long poem, "Mr. Mu Zhang Ying," are all true to the man's experience, which I learned during frequent dinners with his family. I have changed his name.*

## Day's End: A Foreigner Jogs into the Fields

I swoop by the
cricket thin beancurd man slow motion doling
curd to his customers. He gives me the
thumbs up for "smelting health with exercise"
and I slip by the chimney stacks,
old, sooty noses above the
hovels. Now I

am
by the
furrows. Star black
spiders inch through the dust and the weeds burn
green. The buttes green above the plain.
The ancient China giant soon
teems with corn.

I climb
past saplings gorged with buds
and skirt the gravemounds crowded by
goats as ravenous as their goatherd is
quiet.

Every dusk,
I gaze down at the
city—factories, the tenements.
Emptiness

I once believed raged there
like Jeremiah crying for a resurrection is
mischief.

I'm subject to
the machinations of the spring.

## The Dawn Is

a welder's flame
in shadows flung
out of a maze
of steel.

I scrape aside
iron plate doors
and inch out in-
to the day. A
mule cart erupts
with rust but strikes
a lightning pose.
The duckpond sunk
in cinders burns,
copper shards.
Even the dead
pig showered with
lime helps me see.

    The far
refineries gleam
down tv antennas
of tenement rows
above the river
flats where water
birds rustle like
laughter.

  Hooves,
iron shod, churn
up the hard tar
market road and
scrape up sparks like
saws whining through

diamonds. They haul
a cart of crabs
strapped to ice.
Fresh, the food
writhes.

An ancient man
lifts the sun to
his lips, puffs up
flames lighting his
wooden mask face.
His thumb knocks back
a balance, weighs
out my nine eggs.
He says, "Last week,
a hawk swooped near
my pigs. That's bad.
Young man, take these
four free eggs and
repair my broken
luck."

   A girl
opens a shack
to hawk dried meat.
She yawns though the
sun's red like a
tiger's snarl.

   The leap
and claws of light
prowl into the
market stalls
crooked like
cripples and
jumbled where
nothing admits
to being stalked

by newborn
radiance.

The old
man and I frown
over the grave
clickthud of free
eggs he puts with
the bought.

# Mr. Mu Zhang Ying

1. September, 1985

"My young American, drink. I'll tell you the truth.
I translated platitudes at state banquets. Drink.
I worked for one Mr. Smelly, a British Petroleum imperialist.
He smelled. My salary was the fragrance.
Follow my lead. Drink.
Another?
Good.
My young friend, listen. I
was big. I
paid the price.

"Doesn't compare to Hong Kong whiskey?
All the way to Hong Kong for a Christian education—
The priests got me before I was old
enough to corrupt myself.
The rosary, the bread, the wine,
I did it all as a Catholic School of America kid.
I befriended sons of American businessmen.
My English surpassed my mother tongue.
It paid. Real interpreters, rare.
Money, social rank, women, mine.

"Drink to my city, Port Arthur, the pearl.
That's right. The pearl of the Orient it was called.
It was not the slum it has become.
Our overlords? The Japanese.
They brainwashed our children with illiteracy
learned in Japanese. In school we had to use Japanese.
Of course many of us failed. The Japs called us stupid.
They were intelligent. They began World War II.
How did they manage that?
China, all of it, had to be theirs.
They forced me translate their propaganda.

Heads of rebel Chinese hung from the city hall gate.
Everyday, fresh, new heads assured us of the rigors of Japanese
civilization. They told me to translate their propaganda.
I'm no hero. I wrote.
I hacked out reams of their propaganda.
Besides, they underpaid so
I wrote, 'Please, Mr. Yankee, surrender.
Our food's much better than yours.
Surrender and our wives will teach you how to cook.'
You don't believe? This same note
the Japanese kamikazied on you at Midway.
This same note detonated, an atom bomb.
Clever bunch, you Americans, you used it,
my note, for toilet paper.

"You're too young to know.
What do you know about love?
Fight with one, dance with the other.
Kept divorce rates low.
What do I mean? I mean two wives at once.
'House, food, wife: America, China, Japan.'
This proverb explains the three good things.
American house? I was rich—mine on Shady Lane.
Chinese food? No problem. I'm Chinese.
Japanese wife? Illegal.
What is that word? Oh, yes, miscegenation.
The Japanese authorities were afraid of miscegenation.
Mixing Chinese and Japanese blood?
Forbidden upon pain of death.
Bribes were not forbidden.
I bought out the entire Japanese administration.
She, my Japanese wife, laid out my clothes just so.
At breakfast she'd wait, ready to butter my toast.
What else? When the Japanese surrendered, she left.

"My devastation was not complete.
It was the civil war that completed my devastation.
The Communists now call the civil war the

Communist revolution. They call it glorious.
The victors write the histories and will not acknowledge that both sides
inflicted a lot of wrong.
The Communists won. I lost.
The victors reviled the rich, educated slobs
like me. I still floated on the top.
Yesterday's cream is today's scum.
To avoid guilt by association,
my Chinese wife took my son. They fled south.
I worked a factory assembly line for seventeen years.
I put together sewage pumps.
It didn't ruin my charm.
I married another, a genius, a dentist.

"The 1960s brought the Cultural Revolution.
Whatever culture it had in it, I don't know.
Boot lickers and peasants, suddenly top dog.
My new wife and daughter and I were shipped away
for reeducation to the northern countryside.
My education reached completion up there.
Years I learned how to shovel out pig sties.
I earned a PhD in pig sty dynamics.
"After class, I paraded down the village lanes.
I wore a dunce cap scrawled with
characters broadcasting my crimes.
Any refusal to parade would have taught a bullet to
reeducate my skull.
The children threw rocks.
They spat.
I'm lighthearted, otherwise I'd be dead.
My wife died.

"Too late for her when the Communists gave up on culture.
Now it's China to be a supermarket just like America.
That's good.  really think it is for the good.
To develop the government needs English.
So? Me, I know English.

The government said, 'You're rehabilitated.
You're now a professor, department chairman.
Be grateful.' I'm big again.
The pay's good.

"My new wife and I,
What good are we together?
We just creak and moan all day.
She can cook and I can eat.
As for the rest, we're too old.

"Whiskey? Enough whiskey.
Young one, sip this tea, ginseng tea,
a tonic, soothes, makes you light, like youth.

"Drink."

2. January, 1986

"Eat.
You're not fat.
What a time I've had, making excuses to the administration.
'Why isn't he fat?' they ask. I tell them you're neurotic.
Eat. Eat more.
Here. The mushrooms and pork have always been your favorite.

"You should have married a Japanese.
My Japanese wife? Her world was my oyster.
Chinese were banned from the great dance halls
but I'd pass for a Japanese with my better wife.
I'd stroll through all the foreigners' clubs,
buying up all the whiskey.
Of course my Chinese wife bore me a son.
For that I am grateful.
But ask her to dance? I wouldn't dare.

"My Japanese wife would wear a kimono, pouting when I went to work.
It took a world war to drive her away.

The Russians invaded. Some fates are worse.
I translated for a general of theirs.
You didn't know I knew Russian?
It was easy after English and Japanese.
But a spy, a friend of mine, accosted me right in the general's office.
He wanted me to join up with the capitalists and spy.
I told him, 'Get way from here, it is too dangerous.'
Only a little money I accepted from him, out of friendship.
When the Russians got him they used torture.
He singled me out.
I didn't deserve the concentration camp.

"Don't look so stricken.
Eat. Your heart is too tender.
Eat this chicken basted in turtle broth.
It's flavored with the bark of the cinnamon tree.
If you knew Siberia, you'd gorge.
Lard some flab onto those ribs.
You might need the
fat tomorrow.

"To stimulate your appetite, I'll tell you the truth.
Up in Siberia, our spitting contests were Olympic.
Even in April, your spit freezes before it hits the ground.
I was no common laborer. I worked at a
desk, translating their Russian orders however foul
into plaintive Chinese. The soldiers fed me more
than the others. That kept me alive.
The soldiers needed me alive.
They needed me to keep the concentration camp orderly.
They needed me to keep riots from breaking out.

"Mao and Stalin got along in those days.
Mao agreed to take me back.
I was glad to return to civilization.
Did the Maoists greet me with rum and butter cake?
No. They herded me and all the other returning prisoners
into a stadium. They taught us a moral lesson.

A skull for a skull.
The stupid fool pounded a nail into his mother's skull.
His lover didn't want mama to be one of the wedding presents.
When the bullet hit his skull,
he was kneeling before twenty thousand.
Deserved it.

"I did the only sane thing.
I wrote fourteen hundred pages of confession—
so tedious, all about my bourgeois tendencies.
Every line was criticized by my confessor.
I polished it down to nine hundred pages.
Who wants to go through life by rewriting the
annals of one's stupidity?
Actually, I had hope.
They thought a young dog could learn new tricks.
They released me. I was twenty-seven, fit for employment.
I was assigned a place on a factory assembly line
but I was single, bait
for post-war widows. I found one
I'd humbly accept. I was nothing, but, she, a
dentist. She could ravage the most jaded man.
Our girl, skin like her mother's.
We wanted a son.
The '58 Great Leap Backward—
for grain, my wife had to drill many favors.
The famine. After that, she couldn't get pregnant.
We managed to live with that.
But the Cultural Revolution—
you know our time in that village killed her.

"Remember: the
Earth belongs to the living.
My wife was dead, but I had to live.
For pocket money, I kept a rabbit hutch.
Their noses were always excited.
Delicious, an income, enough to spare change for my daughter.
Up there in the northern countryside, wielding a scythe,

she wailed, harvesting. I took away the scythe.
She wasn't okay until she married that country bumpkin.
She's still up there, caring for her children.
She's visiting next month.
You're expected for dinner.

"So what if I am a professor? Eleven years of
berating my colleagues for their atrocious grammar.
I'm tired of it. I'm retiring.
I'm going to make a fortune.
We old professors are gathering heads.
We're raising prawns for the Japanese market.
I'm the translator.

"Eat these dumplings.
They're the meal's climax.
But, don't hurry.
When they're cold, my wife will reheat them.

"I admit, the way you eat, it's remarkable."

3. June, 1987

"Why don't you have children?
When you're over for dinner, I feed you sea cucumbers.
They're expensive. They're aphrodisiacs. They're failing.
Without children, you'll have no son.
Sons can be useful. Sometimes they reappear.
My son offered to let me live with his
children, sons of my firstborn son.
A year, enough time to mollify the dead.
A year his mother's been dead.
Last time I held him, he babbled, 37
years ago. His mother always was politically astute.
She abandoned me, knowing what I'd endure.
I told my son, 'Your mother's fleeing?
That was good. I was shipped north.
Had you been with me, you would have endured the north.'
"I'm a university chairman but I'm broke.

Inflation's ruining me.
Our dragon economy—I'm destitute.
Rejoin my son? I'll need hospital care he must pay?
No. I'll stay here
and suffer.

"Don't fidget like that.
You're late for class but here are the facts.
Your students are flirting now to get engaged and
procreate during the honeymoon.
The sooner the child, the sooner the benefits.
Your child will work while you laze around during your
dying days. Let your students be. Be late.
My son embodies filial piety—
that's the word, piety.

"Why are you listening to an old man when you should be in class?
You're late for class. I'll scrawl out this excuse for you.
Have somebody read it to the class.
Just remember your duty tonight.
I'll be the godfather.
Don't worry.
I'll name your first son Patience, son of Tardy.
Get to class."

4. August, 1988

"Cheer up.
It's sunny, like my days north when I was spared the whip.
Men were used like mules to pull the plows through ice and mud.
Lift weights. Take up pole vaulting.
One who survived had been a pole vaulter during his
Harvard days. Enough meat left on him to do the
mule's job while the American influence drained away like his
muscles while we starved. When your
government sentences you to the Dakotas as a
communist sympathizer, you'll need your muscles then.
"You're getting sentimental.
Numb yourself.

Before your train's gone, we have a few minutes.
This locomotive, take a lesson from it.
When it starts off on a long journey home,
its wheels spin out from the load it drags behind
but then it grips the rails and it goes.
Be this locomotive.
Go.

"Up in the Dakotas, get drunk with the local peasants.
Get so drunk you'll weep out the truth.
Tell them of your fame in China, the news clips,
your bit part in that tv movie. Brag
about your pay, how you could afford fresh mushrooms.
Deliver the peasants the facts.
With them drink so hard you can't help but tell the truth.
The next day the peasants will act like they've forgotten what
you said. But they won't forget.
They'll be charmed.
I charmed peasants like this.
They didn't spare me the harness.
They spared me the whip.

"Don't be stupid.
Change with the political winds.
After all, you've jogged into the countryside everyday.
You've grown strong. You'll thrive in America.
You'll get a job.

"Save money.
Save enough for the airfare. Return.
Weed it. Leave a tearjerking poem on it.
What? My gravemound.
So—my death. I've lived. My life went well enough.

"Go.
The conductor's whistled.
      "Stock up on bourbon.
My ghost will be malignant unless there's bourbon.

I assure you it has to be the best of Kentucky bourbon.
We'll say our same old jokes when my ghost visits you.
We'll drink to each other's health then.

"Get
on the train.

"Humor will bear your grief."

# Visiting an Abandoned Buddhist Monastery's Painted Cave

My flashlight drills the altar full of radiance.
Mold's graffiti splashes up a dusk
of wall. Voices cry out. No one is there.
Gods crumble, sandstone to my touch
I brush away a mural's grime.
A prince eases before a tiger.
The animal bites open the human's intestines.
The royal hands grip light,
fingers playing a
musical wind.
Out of the wind, a Goddess walks.
Brittle halo, tin, she weeps into her hands.
The tiger ravages the lungs and ribs.
Jade burns the gleam through shadow.
Wrists flash out silver.
Gore rivers fangs.
Limestone on fire, sticks become waters,
blessing, patriarchs
frenzy.
Within the tiger's jaws, the man hears a
flute purge, a gong alarm,
a melody of wings.

The sacrifice fulfills the spring.

# Helping the Birth Along

Noon rays hook shadows down my nose,
knifepoints down my lip, a bandit's grin.

The bees could be my tongue in a girl's ear.
The wings play, rioting in many blossoms.

I lounge up in a flowering peach tree.
I'm chewing springs of May new grass.

My hands twitch, fingering an amulet.
My prayers must help the birth along.

Mother's spasms thundered, whirling me
away from home and into this tree.

A pierce in Mother's voice hurled me away.
It out-thundered thunder, anvils hammering.

I know all about the pain and the afterbirth.
I know all about the weeping and the stillbirth.

I want a living brother I'll
lead like a soldier

through pond muck, our thighs burbling through the slime.
We'll snatch up frogs and hurl them beyond the sun—

to unearth cat bones,
teaching a brother to run his palm along the fangs—

I and a living brother will fly my tiger kite.
It will claw away the thunder and the lightning.

It will out roar storms, tall in prowl and hunger.
Its surge will snatch us up and we will soar,

witnessing a paradise of fields and harvest.  No,
my kite's not just a winking penny-like in wind.

I'll no longer know the weeping and the stillbirth.
This time my new brother will be born alive.

# Toward Dawn, a Construction Worker Bulldozes a Freight Yard's Coal Mountain

The treads grip, spurring the blade on.
So what if I rattle in the fumes—the dust.
I'm one with the night sky and loom
too near the precipice.
Ease down the brakes.
Stall out.
Damn headlights die.
Far floodlamps pierce my eyes.
The freight yard rails turn radiant below.
Arteries sprawling through my breasts,
nerves sewn up my tongue, long rusted out
unlike this yard I
serve.

                    I
crawl with tons of steel on my back.
The throttle's full. First gear grinds in.
The treads heave, the blade bites in.
Wave after wave of coal hurls back.
They break onto oceans of ebony.
My machine rips away the world.
Full above springs the harvest moon.
Mooncakes will be mine at dawn.
The stars issue their commands I
always disobey.

   Old whiskey nosed
husband sleeps with a bottle instead of
me, rots like the trash fishwives won't sniff.
Whipped him with a dishrag, cried, "Hell. Flames. Fire. Flee."
I lit a match and burnt his big toenail black.
That didn't wake him, troll
unconscious again.

Mother called dawn
the magpie soaring into our yard, the thief
snatching away the stars' ruby necklace tonight.
Mother read me fairytales about this magpie who
stole the bittern's wife. He squawked to her so tunefully
she grew to love him for it.

The dawn, that fool
dressed up in tatters, gulping moonshine like it's rice wine,
dares beam throughout the freight yard and all the downtown tow-
ers.
He leans on my cab, drumming his fingers, wanting me
to cook him breakfast. He is dazzling
the factory skylights, broken—the streets,
torn mud lanes, this my
dawn in frost
shadows.

It is beginning daylight.

# The Dark, the Death, the Dog, the Dawn, the Popsicles

The dark,
ancient, black and white footage,
scratched, an old, forgotten movie panning away from
mazes of barb wired brick walls, panning further on out and
revealing neighborhoods of hovels crowded on a poor city's edge.

Famine
pinching its ribs, a dog shirks away
from four brothers shouldering their mother like pallbearers to the
hospital.
The dog does not care that the mother has already died.
The dog does not care that the four glance up,
priests waiting for the dawn to call
them into worship.
The brothers tramp away,
a boney monotony. The dog eyes them no longer.
It paws a garbage can, nosing the lid
away, a clattering
annunciation.

The old black and white film runs out.
Dawn brings technicolor, a silk dragon scarf
cowled around her skull, wild, the lion designs on
her padded jacket:
Shriveled,
warped into rainbow angles, a
crone yowls, *"Shway gao! Shway gao!* (Snow cakes! Snow cakes!)
Every household for blocks around wakens to her cry.
*"Shway gao! Shway gao!"* She limps,
hawking popsicles.

A girl sprints,
a dime almost bouncing off her thumb.
She buys two vanilla, tossing one to the
dog, eating the other.
The crone scolds, "That's a waste of a good popsicle."

The girls snails, dawdling
like forever could not be enough time to delay going home.

The dog gobbles.
It licks its chops.

The crone heaves up her bag, swaggering,
yowling on.

## An Old Woman Chops Wood

My ax cracks down
and the wood bursts clean. I
hurl piece enough to wedge death's skull
to the darkbound ass cart. Death, turn
tail and flee before I skin you for my meat.
You raked my husband's lungs with cancer.

Dead drunk, you staggered into the funeral.
You greeted the old dustdevil, my husband's soul.
Together you laughed away into God knows what.
My husband didn't even
wave goodbye.

In my arms I took my one grandson and
sang him songs of Tibetan leopard bones,
snow leopard bones to grant us immortality—
slices of leopard bones stuck into the boy's lunch.
Snow leopards leave pawprints of the unseen,
hardest to see of all the animals of immortality,
camouflaged against the snow like snow
is all there is to see.

For my grandson I'll carve this wood with runes
and draw the cormorant hex through the script.
I see the living shadow of
my husband in his face.

I'll live to see five great grandchildren named.

## Sundown Quiet

Emeralds in tar,
facets spark May
out of the sun

lowering through
ululations of
goats

butting horns, leaping
hoof dance up a path
in rows of new corn,

beards forking rays
from the dying
radiance,

their barrel ribs
hooping wine-
skin bellies,

teats gorged with milk
full like balloons
about to pop,

cliffside gleam
and mica shine,
their eyes.

Their bleating cries
alive the
quiet.

# *from* Kyoto Uncollected Poems (1989–2002)

## Kyoto Temple Night

Tigers
wake. They stretch.
They sniff. They growl.
They leap and prowl
the wind on claws
of sky.

A whip
of dragon scales
flails its folds
on folds of fangs
unfurling a tail's
lash and writhe
out thundering
the sky.

Birch
shelter the
moss on stone
lanterns lit
within the light
snowfall tonight.

Raked
sand mimes
oceans of no
sound where no
waves hit the no
boulders of the
no shores of the
isles of the
blest.

My love,
walk with me here.

## Lynched Crow

—Found in a Kyoto Mountain Vegetable Garden

Gallows humor, rusty pole
lynch pin gibbet for a crow
hung up, stiff—the ebon jester
yawns alive a rare bird's gape
bored to tears below the blue
sky, the tongue a circus moon's

tin, a skull of tin foil moons,
birdbrains, the dance the pole
upholds within this garden blue
where dawn light makes this old crow
scarecrow its brethren with a gape
gregarious, a turncoat jester,
a tattletale.

        Winging it, the jester
puppets a prance, a jig of moons
arabesque, a grand jeté gape
the breeze bumps about the pole—
a ballerina, not a crow,
primadonna aloft, blue.

Death's a richly fabled blue
tapestry the foppish jester
dons in laughter, a naked crow
dressed to kill in wings of moons,
a fashion victim, the North Pole.
The corpse dangles, an Arctic gape.

With furrowed brow, the doctor's gape
expands to expound on his blue
ideas about the central pole.
He sings unsung cause, a jester
jailed for life, a prison moon's
jailbird, a forgotten crow.

Some mother' son, this choked up crow
masked in jade, this sardonyx gape
joys to know that at last nine moons
rise and heave soul out of the blue
cap and bells, a rhinestone jester
doomed for a time to grace the pole.

A scarecrow crow crows, "Gape. Eat crow."
The moon's rise, pink, hung from a pole,
the jester dawns. The radiance is blue.

# Tanka

Tar, grit, herons reach
for flight where cliffs scorch and a
shroud splinters the sky

There a kiln-fired clay bowl meets
lips breathing in flower tea

## The Chupacabra

Water light and rippling up the wet
nightfall branches, my love stole
glimmers from the dying sun. We fell
into the tapestry of our night's knowing.
We clothed each other in our sacred cries.
Our horns hooked scarlets from the dark.
We gorged on the blood-thick petals.
We cooed, far from the stench
called men.

            They snared my love.
   By her horns they roped her down.
She snarled and hissed but they darted her quiet.
Destiny: The city zoo.
Caged,
my love perches. Crowds flock to the new display.
My love chirps, begging for food.
Like a chickadee she nods, forgetting what she was.
Alone I wander through fire scarred valleys.
Char and fumes follow where men torch the petals.
Goats pasture on the weeds where flourished my
paradise.
       The goats
   scatter pell-mell
the nights I claw into their pens.
I seize and wrench their spines.
I take them by the throat.
I suck them dry.

       Tonight I rip a human throat,
   finding and fumbling the zoo keys.
Barred by the moonlight and the fertile dark,
huddled, my love
reeks. Her cage door I bang open, a crash

to kill the prison silence. She does not know me.
Forgetfulness suffered by the tame afflicts her.
So weak, she lets me carry her away.
Police sirens follow our every crouch.
My leaps huge and out of breath—
the city fades, electric glare
giving way to
cliffs
and valleys,
orchid covered mountains.
      Snarls leap
out of the leafy glimmering.
Hunger chirrups. Need sings.
Tangles of vines web our slow
clambering into slopes
all but impassable.
Downpour erupts and
hits our fur like
lightning.
Like infants cling, my love holds me.
Yowls
guide our way to a ravine
where a spring births streams.
Down cliffside steeps to the
purest waters I
carry my
love.
Filth,
bark-like, her underbelly
I cleanse, clawing
gravel up her ruined fur.
The water shocks her into memory.
She has no need to speak.

Water light and rippling up the wet
nightfall branches, we gorge on the
blood thick petals. We coo,
far from the stench
called men.

# A Bat Addresses All of Humanity

"Nor you nor I will ever die
when rodent wings can soar on high,
mere mammal wings of skin and fur
out whirling when the whirlwinds hurl
my swirl twirl up and I write my
signature way across the sky.
    'What's this?' I hear you humans cry,
'Nor you nor I will ever die?
You flap your flips to flit and eat.
Flutter on. You're nothing fleet.
You need food, and that means death
licks away your rodent breath.'
    I'm sick of cant.
I'll listen not to human rant.
Fools, I have got a few bat facts
to give your mortal snorts the ax.
My ears cup out and catch my second sight
beaming back detailed maps of the night.
My sonar brains provide the guide
to ways beyond my rodent plight.
I see, I hear. My birthright's right.
O, humans, I'm of caves and dirt
but dart above toward second birth
where the love I wing is
endless mirth.
My cursive's bold. I dot the I.
My signature means seek to find.

My laughter's all Sir Death can bite."

# Three Songs of the Animals

*The Bear*

Bumblebees my fangs nip while my tongue lips
the honey and the wax out of the hive
wholesome up the old oak. I heave
my claws while my slide crawls in. My lick laps
the life out of a house and home. The leaps
of rage gouging their stings to blind me have
dive bombed. I itch. I grin and won't behave.
I leave it a war zone, honey. My lopes
rumble away, fat haunched. But, my nose? Wise.
It has caught your scent far within a grove,
fragrance more than the lilies of all songs
flowering within the wettest of wet dawns,
the rain-soaked fur of you, my love.
Bear my ways.

*The Hummingbird*

I whip my ruby rash
lightning lash down limbs of pine
shadows. Shuddering up, I twine
my quips down forest lips and dash
out of a sun ray while my splash
in thighs of petals mirrors shine
on pollen. Fruit, the flower's wine!
I chant my wings, I chirr my thrash,
My buzzball act, a half wept tear
poised to fall, steady.
Dangling, I test
the nectar: My needle beak, blest,
sings in. No ornament, no shame,
I spear
beauty.
I pollinate the flame.

*The Worm*

Birdbrains to brain me, jackdaw jaws to rout
me into Heaven early, thrush jabs damn
near plucking me out—
What a dumb
worming toward doom must my wriggling rate
when men take to their spades? My life's a rut?
The fishing hook desired? Nope. My dim
crumbling good soil for gardens munches dame
earth. My appetites allow me to root
in earth. My slow blind climb to nowhere is
content with helplessness. My tender head
parts earth in ways so whole no man
could ever equal me for all my bliss
digesting life. My mouth takes hold.
All goes to plan.
I eat a path
thickening me, my health.

## Los Angeles Evening

Dusk's smith
tongs up the molten sun,
slams it down, hammers,
bangs spark after spark
up from the city's rim.

The smith eyes
their darkening prize,
the iron's hissing edge, the sun
they thrust into the ocean right
where waves drop into the new night.

## 寂, sabi

War
ice
Plains of snow
Tanglings of barbed wire
Trenches, endless          Where harvests were
fields of wheat, not men          This earthenware
teacup, a glaze
of grays,
寂,sabi, the beauty of all that is
mangled,
cold

Frost
dawn melts lost
nighttimes off the least
temple twig          The raked sands,
fingerprints of divinity,
identity's
trace,
patterns of a better truth,
these teacup grays          寂,sabi, the beauty of all that is
unspoken,
hidden

Char
in flames          A firepit
A mountain shelter, fumes
A face, a rock cliff
Many canyons and summits, her hands
reach out to the fire          Outside, wind,
snow          These teacups grays,
寂,sabi, the beauty of all that is
hermitage,
refuge.

Withered
fingers crouch
above a wheel The slouch
Time's mask, the face Bent to her task,
the hundred-and-one-year old potter,
acclaimed at last
This exhibit,
hers 寂,sabi, an intelligence,
the beauty of all that is quiet joy

## The Spelunker's Death

My helmet beam, the only light,
I grope on my hands and knees.  Cold
rushes up like a god's been killed.

I grip the tunnel and worm in,
struggling to reach a happy grace
where water down the sacred earth
hollows a path
        but what's beneath
me's crumbling, become a pit.
My helmet beam falls down the pit.
Far down, it fades into a point.

Blind touch to give my fingers sight,
the granite's rough I read like braille,
alphabets singing of the brawl
so ancient it all appears again
within myself, whether to dare,
whether to go on and endure
this escape from the day to light
alive a way out of my lot,
to do so now, or be too late,
too old or dead tomorrow.

My feet and fingers fail to grip.
The pit's edge I cannot grasp.

    I'm falling, bonfires full
of cries, earth odors, the clean, hid-
den veins of water, the air's hold
of lips and hair, fragrance of
shale, sheaves of winter wheat,
time oozing from last light,
        a fault

in bedrock singing of a wind
without end.

I'm hitting bottom
where starlight and time
are dead.

I bleed the dark's own gleam.
My wounds ooze shadows down the gloom.

The dark
illuminates my fall from light,
my death in earth, my sacred lot.

# Why Rhyme?

Why rhyme? Hear the gong's bong of two as one,
no clang's bang, but the brass and brash of song.
Admit free verse will always be outsung.

Electrify your startling. Do not shun
the rite of two as one. Dare right the wrong.
Why rhyme? Hear the gong's bong of two as one.

Without rhyme, lyrics breathe with but one lung
and even that's collapsing, a wheeze of song.
Admit free verse will always be outsung.

If music makes you tick, go tock the hung
man with a push—and laugh. You've done no wrong.
Why rhyme? Hear the gong's bong of two as one.

The hanged man, Tommy Rhymeless, has no tongue.
His dangling silence, his one and only song.
Admit free verse will always be outsung.

Tommy Rhymeless swings while chimes well flung
from the ideal harmonize. Sing. Belong.
Why rhyme? Hear the gong's bong of two as one.
Admit free verse will always be outsung.

## *from* A Dunce Cap Gorged with Kyoto Quasi Petrarchan Sonnets

My wife and I left Jinzhou, China, in 1988, travelling to Kyoto, Japan in search of both employment and adventure. It was a jarring, often exhilarating change from a quiet and calm, though poor, basically agricultural country, where the Communist government gave everyone a job and a salary along with housing and medical insurance. Thrust into capitalist hurly-burly Japan, we were on our own. Anxiety and uncertainty afflicted us as we struggled to find jobs and housing. Life in a beautiful and culturally rich city rewarded our efforts. We stayed for seventeen years.

While Kyoto's sensualness is evident by a glance at the city's myriad temple gardens, one thing little-known outside of Japan is the folks' humor. Whimsical lightheartedness, complete with a total lack of irony, no sarcasm and little satire, this kind of comedy prevails in Japan, as they do in these poems.

The book is one long poem, split up into quasi-Petrarchan sonnets held together by a narrative. The action takes place in twenty-four hours. This selection follows the story. At times, three asterisks *** pop up. These signify a break, where I jumped to a point further on in the narrative.

# By Kyoto's Kamo River, Fox Hunts Down Clown

Lark, spark, Fox bounds out of the dark.
She pierces the air, her flame after
flame lunging to the shores in laughter
for Clown. She slinks up to his cheek-
y Charleston chumpish on the bleak
dawn edge of waters. She sniffs the cur.
Her nose writhes. She gags, tries to purr,
sneezes, swears baths had better mark
that stench with sense, dares re-sniff, roars,
nips his heel, flattens by a stone.
Clown yipes, calls the bite the breeze,
rubs his hoof, hums at the dawn shores,
chirps, "Nope.  Nobody. I'm alone."
To propose, the fool will fall on his knees.

## Clown, Eventually, Beholds the Trail of Cakes Fox Plunks Down

Clown clucks, "Weird! My weird's weird. I hear
how hunger's hollowed out my belly—
such drastic gastric groans. For jelly
cakes crammed raspberrily, I'd sear
in Hell. Weird. O, my weird, I FEAR
I'M VICTIM of the truest telly
visions gone digital, swell, sweet
fantasias." The hound howls, rears
up and sniffs out the trail Fox-beat-
en by the cakes, leaps to the scent,
wolfs down one, druffs up the next.
Hound whines, slurping on fleet feet
fleeing the waters, a nose bent
on breakfast.

# Fox's Trail of Cakes Lures Clown into Inari, the Fox Shrine

Around priests glaring like rocks at
his carnival, Clown cartwheels by
their raking sand designs of why
what is is. The fool tumbles flat
in altars, cocks an ear, hears rat-
atat tats like tanks, drools at sky-
clear saké sacrified to pry
luck from the Gods. The brat
laughs as he lips quaint quips and rips
up pompoms of his dunce cap, heaps
them as an offering born to cheat
at death's odds, prays in hopes
death's dead.

***

# Fox and Clown Wander toward the Temple's Garden Pond

All arm in arm the lovers leap
laughbound, flirting on, chuckling low
but dumbstruck now, they gawk in slow
wordless wonder where pines sweep
their boughs on away into deep
dissolve, mirrors of pond,
the Buddha's glow.
        Fox tugs Clown's toe
to jolt him, joys, "Try, think. Think. Weep
upon the meanings." Clown knuckleknocks
his noggin, wiseguy peeps at the
pond, mut howls at the water's rippling.
He croons, "I need shots on the rocks
soon." Fox plants a grave growl and a
kiss up his neck.
        He's giggling.

## Clown Sees Fox in the Temple Pond's Reflection

In the pink, she blinks winks and eases
on shore lawn, dawns a yawn while her
silks mink their crinkling to sheen's lure
lithe, beauty's pure cure. That fact teases
Clown. He coughs out wowed warble sneezes,
snorts, "My snore's snuffed by how her
daemon gathers in the water's
stir, a nymph aflame. That pleases
who? Come live with me and be
my love." Her reply, "I will live
with thee and be thy love," buds
rose his mug. He's blushing! She
operas, "O, my love, I'll give
thee coral clasps and amber studs."

***

## Fox and Clown Enter a Corporate Skyscraper's Lobby

Man's manling's manling, marmalade,
Clown mourns, "Corpse in a corporate
morgue, I limp like a half dead rat
begging for bread. To make the grade,
to get a job"—The lobby's staid
fake old Greek sculptures blunt
him to tears. Shunt,
whir, flash by: a huge mobile made
of cartoon characters. . .

        The lobby's monied, sheer
abstraction, a wall mural, *Bull
And Woman Making a Monster's Day
Of Birth,* a splatter of blood and mere
housepaint—Clown oooos, "It's beautiful."
Fox gawks, knowing not how she'll slay.

## In the Elevator, Clown and Fox Rise

"The whirligig
of time tornados away my
cap and bells, hurls me, litter by
the waysides where I bop a jig
jitterbugged to win this twig-
ripe, this girl, wind friend, thigh
of thrum and blood for whom I will try
to win work," he thinks.
She thinks, "Big-
wig or not, jobbed or not, bucks to
burn or bust to bum, my fool will
millionaire my love. O, love's thrill
out-throstles nightingales. Chirps woo
in calls of harmony, the Song of Songs,
an aviary at dawn, where Clown belongs."

## The Fox God, the Boss, Reviews Clown's Resume

"You have to right to remain
silent. Everything you don't
say can and will be held against
you," proclaims the boss in insane
intonations. Clown's brains sprain,
popping, a jack-in-the-box benched
in back corner cobwebs, wrenched,
twangling springs. . .

The god's words reign
down, "Outrageous! Optimal!
Graduated *summa cum*
*hilaritatae* out of the States'
United Institute of Bull
and Career Clowning, you're, in sum,
hired."

# The Fox God Growls,

"If pregnancy strip Fox down to
kitchenware, you're canned dead meat I'll
eat," weeps the God in crocodile
tears. "Isn't her figure the woo
too wild to waste on puff like you
clowns?" He stifles a guffaw while
opening the door. Clown sees Fox fil-
ing away prophet reports to
fulfill her office as the boss's
secretary.
            Clown can't repel
the lure of Shivers Regal. He chug-
alugs a bottle, gags up his losses,
gasps, "What the hell, love is compel-
ing me to down this cockroach stuff.
It beetles down my throat. Bugs bug
            me."

            ***

# Clown's Soul Washes Up on the Shores of Hell's Entrance

Not quite a scene off Dante's page
where no one knew so many weep,
crossing on into Hell—the drip
of tears and the faltering enrage
Clown. He kicks them aside. No cage
of dulled desire, he claws in, seethes
to the forefront where the damned cleave
to Charon's raft. They crowd the wage-
hungry old miser, proffering Scar-
let Express Cards. They beg the crony
to turn a blind eye as he types
in credit checks—he's bored!—to bar
unworthies' crossing. "Here's no baloney,"
Clown notes.
    "What I have to put up with," Charon gripes.

# Charon's Checking Clown's Credit

Charon cheapskates a frown
frumpish before Clown's somersault,
leaping on board. The miser's caught
smiling to think the fool might hound
Hell. He chuckles, an old grump bound
to growl at Clown's, "Your ferry's fault-
ed, sir. Is it merry? Nope. Not
one whit. Fix it." The miser's glower
thunders in triumph, trumpets out
Clown's credit report, "It's bad! Sheep
in wolf's clothing, go live in Lamb
and snore, you bore." Clown spouts a pout
but Charon boots the lout out. "Creep,
you're a joke. Scram."

***

# Clown Falls from the Office Tower,

sobs, "When love's river flamed in first
light, sparkly burned the copper dawn
in crucibles molten to lavadoom
death. Was a form of desire's thirst,
dying of love thirst, our love of burst
grapes to wine, groaning. Let her song
arms knead whoever with hugs long
and mushy where, no, not one cursed
truth afflict her. Let my love win
at love, finding love though I die,
splat."
Snow feathers fowl
but plucky stab out of his skin.
They unfurl wings and flap hard, fly-
ing flimsily up.
He's turned into a snowy owl.

# Fox Gains in Courage

Witness to Clown's wing-ed wonder
whirling up and away, O, she
throws the sky grins as if the sea
thunders down and rips asunder
her lungs, dragging her under,
scattering her corpse where an oil-free
coral reef teems with clownfish. "We
suffer rebirth," she laughs. "No blunder,
no—RRr GRRR." Rage like death rips through
her claws scratching runes up, down her
desk which spell, "I quit."
Light-
ning's lightning, she flicks on to woo
Clown. Lightning can't begin to strike
like Fox takes on speed, hurtling
beyond the speed of light.

# Nearly Blind in Daylight, Clownowl Tests his Wings

The young swain swoops a loop to loop,
cries heartily, "Whoops," curves out swirl
curls and croons, "Fox, O, my moon full
of harvest radiance, hunt me down. Dupe
all wrong turns. Reveal how you hoop
my wings with hidden hownows. Hurl
me into harder flight, O, pearl,
O, my, O, my
O."
            A goop group
of smokestacks plumes fumes. Clownowl's wise
night eyes blear, blind to the mass wheeze
grave, craven scene. The birdbrain roast-
rams right through it, broils rare and cries
fowl. Scarred to char, he drops and sneez-
es, "The gross national product! This is gross.
    I'm tarred and feathered."

# Fox Weeps, Cured of Amnesia

Her mind reforges light
in memory, bejewels her mind,
remembering old harvests bound
by Goddess hands, Fox Goddess light,
the true Inari, the stalks and the dirt,
boundless rice, the times when Fox found
herself alive, on the hunt, bound-
less leaps, the sprite
she was.
She wails, "The Fox God raped
my mother, raped and kidnapped me
and my kind, brainwashed us to a dull
forgetting.
Clown! I alone have escaped
to sow him, love to reap,
to be."
Off she Clownhunts.
She sniffs.
She leaps.

# To Become a Buddhist Monk, Clownowl Throws

the dead world the stiff upper beak
and streaks toward starkest temples where
monks bend in prayer, snow shadows bare
but petal emptiness there. "Bleak
but lotus, lotus austere, me, the freak
to cloister, seeks to find, wisely to dare
dump the world, to gain the isles fair
in Paradise," Owl clhooaimts while peak
after peak greets his eyes unblind-
ed by the night, the mountains real
in temples gonging chants, a home
to prayer.
        Snowy soars, leaves behind
world's wreckage and all of the dust,
greed and desire.
        His huge wings wheel
away to where Fox awaits him.

## Owl Enters the Garden Where Reigns Kannon, the Goddess of Mercy

Down to the bronze light, evening air
where Kannon, Mercy, holds her water
bowl up for ALL, Owl glides in laughter
to a smooth landing's perch, O, where
calms Kannon, naked soles left bare
to the stream beading them.
            Owl drinks.  After
all, he's parched.  Now a daughter
to Kannon, more water now than fire,
Fox appears, dance out of time!  Owl
brawks, "Augh," and feather leap hop hides
behind Kannon's skirts. Demon shame
broils the bird longing for a towel
to cover his burn scars. Chump pride's
punk, he squirms.
            Fox enters Kannon's pool.

# Clown's a Fool's Fool's Fool's Fool's Fool's Fool's Fool

Dawdling in
Kannon's pool, mercy's flow, Fox bathes
in mercy, boundless waters made
for fools.
She scrubs away her flim-
flam fox tail, defangs her fangs—limbs
she declaws, fur swashed down the path
of mercy's wanderings.
She stirs up wave
after wave, rinses, hums to win
Clown in. "Don't be shy. Loaf in the
pure." Wholly human, love's blood close
in human touch, Fox beckons Clown
to come on in and dip for a
spell. A frail snail, Clown, jello slow,
creeps into his shell, shakes his head
no.

## This Part Needs No Title

Mut by the collar, he's hauled in
by her grip wholly. What sizzboil
steam baths hissspurt while her love toil
cleanses, masseuse dancehands to span
time and remake space for her man
in snowy need.
            Her fingers coil
patsmack his burns. They rub in oil
of essence, scents' sense made to plan
ways to ease suffering and heal
her fool, Clown reborn, become a
man lounging in pure love's unknown
known. The fool yumgroans in the real
reel of his love's touching in the
pool.  A fool and a fox,
     a marriage sown.

## In Kannon's Garden, They Have Snoozed Off

Grace: No mosquitoes dive-
bomb swarm and probe our lovers to
awakening though our duo crew
Edens in nakedness, entwined,
arm in arm, tangled
vines.
No longer fur, but skin, blood who'll
always rule, rising from her woo
won, from nightmares, Fox cries, "Deprive
us? No. Death cannot be. We'll prove
death's dead."
Clown snorts out a grin of
scowls, sits up, howls, "We beat the odds.
Thanks, Goddess. . ." They coo a sighcry
kiss goodnight, squirming back into love's
sleep lands. Why not? Against all odds,
they've one.

# Fox Dreams

Moon's sapphire flames my blood's new rose.
I am unfolding, hunting down him who
takes my lunge and cries, rivering to
love me. My fangs dig in and close.
I mean I've tickled the fool's toes.
My love also knows woes like spews
of sewage, egrets dead who'll woo
bacteria while detergent snows
my stream. Please do not pollute
my stream.
    I have scrubbed my love's burns away.
I have scrubbed him down to a core of man-
dom in clean waters, cure's pure to the root
riot of it, death clash to slay
his husband heat.
        My fool, my fan.

# Clown Dreams

Skinned alive, chicken chortling in
the freezer called space and time, I
freezer-burned to an Arctic sigh
shivering, "Why? Oh, why?"
The protest's bonfire din
died to ash and smoke where I'd been
barbecued alive by Army wise
guys—China's paradise, O my
love. You bejeweled my burning skin
by heaping on fire opals and the moon-
stone bloodstone of all your cat's eye
beauty beautifying my rebirth's life.
A harlequin opal born to dusk jewel
all moonlit laughter, me helped by
you, Fox.
    We'll thrive.

# Fox Dreams

The death moon's black hole bore me. I
leapt from her womb, danced into dawn
like salmon swim back home, not drawn
to slave in office towers.
                                        I
blushed, burned to see the clown light pry
no shadows from me, spirit only, pawn
to wind, wind's chattel, bloodless spawn
to nothing, nothing much, me. That's why
I died in waters and became Clown's wife
to love away in life.
                    I spit on my place
among the stars, rip my constellation from
the sky, desire no consolation for my life
in Clown bloodhard, dirtbound, no outer space
star glory but Clown, laughter, hymn, his hum.

# They Dream On As One Mind Together

Mercy, the miracle: a suicide
falls upward to reverse death's deed
indeed. Indeed, dawn towers bleed
a sign of witness: Alone, a fox bride
unblinds her fingertips, lets them slide
down rocks, stone brail telling her needs
to be undone, rewoven:  to change.
      Love seeds
time, the Fox Goddess, true Inari's stride
through harvest rice, scythe tunes and the
dirt's rebirth, our marriage, the grain
ripe where we reap, rise and sagelight
twirl rageprance water's jig, all a
stream's touch, all a new rain
blooddance in us, the blood
of us.

## *from* Lore

These nine poems are taken from *Lore,* a full-length collection telling of the lives and times of a family adhering to the old hunter-gatherer ways, although they have been conquered by an industrial, imperial nation.

The book has all the hallmarks of prose. It tells a story, seeking to flesh out main characters through landscape, inner monologue and narrative. It also has all the advantages of poetry, working toward achieving a harmony of meaning through concentrated sound and imagery, providing a force of expression not found in prose.

I have selected these nine in order to give an idea of both the narrative and the four main characters, the Warrior, his wife, Sarah, their daughter, Rebecca and her fiancé, Gabriel.

# Sarah Tells Her Daughter a Story

"Opals could not whirl
and spin the way the girl
danced laughter up the night
and played, the very sight
a jewel to all delight.

"When death beheld her games,
he cursed and magicked flames
of lure and sly 'til she
thought she'd leap on and on
in tides of God along.
Into the sea she pranced.
She lipped out gull-like song.
Waves crashing in and the thunder
dragged her in, held her under.

"Death took her drowned
bones but her soul's rebound
out of his grip took flight,
a sparrow gaining height,
soaring with such zing
her feathers had to sing,
"I am I!" It was her cry
remembering the tears and why
her mother blabbered screech
and grovelled while the search
party found her one daughter
washed up out of the water.

    "The sparrow's cry,
'I am I! I am I!'
thundered throughout the sky
even as her call toward
the land took on a chord

like oceans hit by storm.
She dashed to fields and tore
out twigs and weeds. Her soar-
ing back dropped them on shore.
She dashed back, dropping more
twigweed stuff on the shore
again, again, forever
until her flight's endeavor
dams the sea, making death
by drowning simply an
impossibility.

"'I am I! I am I!'
It is love's selfsame cry.

"It haunts the ocean's roar."

# Sarah and the Warrior Pay Witness to their Daughter and the Fox

    Tonight, at clearing's edge,
there prowls the bloody, starlit wedge.
It creeps, slinking through the border hedge.
It sniffs.
            It bounds
like giggles up to our cage of hounds.
Against the bars our curs lash, raving
to rip that free soul fox for misbehaving.
We ask, "Daughter, what do you see?"
"Spirit free,
uncaptured laughter, glee
prancing before the torment of our pups."
Down hammers the cage latch. Our young one gulps
at how like shotgun shot outleap the tongues and yelps
untangling to the chase. Our daughter yells,
"Why do I hear riots of temple bells
out-resounding all our mountain hills
when thunder undams and the lightning spills
the waters of all creation? And why does it blaze a tail
down the nearest forest trail?"
"Why? Why, the fox has just hurtled by."
She cries, "Then why do I see a pack
of wild cards hooked by balls and chains
barreling on to murder?" "Why?
Why the hounds have just bumbled by."
    Far ahead, circling back, the fox hops
on boulders in our meadow stream and whaps
the stones with telltale stench. The first lost hound,
nose down and snuffling up a jackass sound,
bays into sight. The fox leaps a glide
onto the stream's other, higher side,
freezes in a guffaw, seeing how well fried
writhes the hound's nose whirling around to find
the lost, the sacred scent.

"Daughter, what do you see?"
"Wisdom confounds
the soldiers of no fortune floundering in a sea
of dog confusion. But stop asking me.
Parents, what do you see?"
"We see the hounds who've found fox scent.
They swarm about the stream as if victory meant
sniffing and snorting and shaking a wet tail
in triumph for having discovered a false trail.
See there, near the brush, fangs curl up. They leer.
Daughter, that's the fox a stone's throw near."
"I see it. Finally, I do, and the game?
Mine." Arrow after arrow she lets flame.
Each falls away, lost in the brush and dirt.
"What?" our child screams, "It is not hurt?"
The fox stands tall, gives her a glare.
Our daughter dares take on the dare.
She stares back into its vulpine stare.
She sees the fang thick laughter there.
She smells its secret, its birth lair.
She beholds how life, free, abounds.
She cries, "Call off the hounds.
Do as I say or I myself will murder the
dogs. Danger's here, fox. Flee."
We laugh, "No hunt could ever damage thee."

Away the fox and our daughter bound.
Together they trumpet one huntress sound.

They'll hunt each other through the night.

# The Warrior and Sarah Learn of an Engagement

One candleflame provides the witness light.
It lets us behold ourselves, the
light.

                Patience pleads
for a hearing though bone deep sweat beads.
We cannot help but see how starlight bleeds
across our opening door where
two eyes in tears
stare: our daughter brings a hand up to her hair,
draws strands away, leaves her shoulders bare.
For a husband she begged us to let her seek.
Now she's that shriek
crumpled in the door
weeping, "Do you think I am a stone?
Like I'm hard enough to survive life alone?
Like vines
you cleave. Like wines
mix, becoming better by becoming one
in oneness.  Like when the drink's fragrance twines
about the tongue. I mean the taste of love refines
yet you tell me not to yearn for my own.
Your telling me not to seek leaves me torn,
a mouse a shrike impales upon a thorn."
We cry out, "Daughter, go. Find. Adore.
Do not slump here within the starlit door."
She sings, "He and I have already cast dice and found
snake eyes peering up, which means love unbound.
You'll meet him tomorrow. His glance melts ice.
Be prepared. You'll gape twice."

# The Warrior First Meets his Daughter's Fiancé

The Gods could cluck alive a rooster's butt
the way that boy treads puff and glare and strut.
Cocky, he stares hard. His prime prizefight dip
and gobble grabs and we grapple. The pip-
squeak's squeaks squawk. His gasp in my grip
groans. I wrench the boy into the old flip
called Beezelbub's burnt bastard whip,
whirling him down. . .
  Minnow gills, the gasping pup
stumbles to his feet. I help him up.
"Look at me, son. You're only seventeen.
Soon your arms will thicken. You'll beat me clean.
Show me another thing.  Prove me your worth."
He chisels poetry into the drought baked earth.
Poetically burns that boy's thirst for water!
Naturally he wants my only daughter.
"A poet?" I growl, "How
are you skilled with the bow?"
He cartwheels, whooping out a shot
through seventy yards of thicket and a lot
of meadow flowers. I scoff as the arrowhead
thwacks bumblebees, impaling them. "Bees, dead?
"Look, kid, I give you only one more shot."
Like a God he bends his big oaken bow
parallel to his shoulders. He kneels low,
aiming high. "You are going for the sun?
I like that, son. Ambition's good."
Forever he takes steady aim.
No sign of sweat. No hint of strain.
He yawns. Like lightning should,
his release thunders.  The dart flames
into the sun. The light shrieks, bleeds

an early dusk upon the world and flees.
"All right," I cry, "That is enough.
I've got to admit, I like your stuff.
Let us feast. I have good red wine.
Let's toast the marriage. You are fine."

# At his Daughter's Engagement Feast, Drinking Hard, The Warrior Tells a Tale Too Tall To Be Untrue

"Beheaded, yea, I laughed.
Never was I victim of mere mortal fears.
The dying battle crept away in tears.
Night rose. My corpse, abandoned meat,
drew wolves. They licked my smile
but by luck or some god's guile
they left my head alone.

Yips
yowling out of love's infinite
core, snarls growling out of death's starless
roar, my sword cleaving
gore into one heaving
soar:
A hunchback,
a fox-headed priest,
limped out of the night's feast
of stars. I bared my teeth, snarled at the beast.
He cried, "I'm yours from here to forever after.
Idiot, what do you think I am, an elf?
I'm nothing but your worthless, higher self."
I rasped, "Let mange devour you, cur."
He trickled out gobs of laughter,
threw away his head,
thrust my head onto his neck instead,
leapt into the new day,
hurled, cutting apart the battle fray."

## Gabriel, Rebecca's Fiancé

Pig heads on hooks, goat kidney lard pie, men
jostled to grab and gorge on ill-cooked meat.
The marketplace of animals was human. Hate
drove them on. Hunger forced them to buy and eat.
Stench and the rot paid tribute to the August heat.
I sweat blind, cursing my father's stall. The reek—
All day I'd cut and weighed, trimmed out and sold
barnyard flesh to gapes and fangs. Coins of gold
fell from my fingers like fingerprints. Fate
whipped sand into my thirst. I'd worked late.
My father stood at the door. I turned cold.
"I'll disinherit you," he said, "You'll mate
that animal? Her mother has no hand
but a paw. What's that? They pray to the old
Gods but the missionary priests have banned
it. Son, that family sacrifices to the Earth.
Remember what you are. Recall your worth.
Bad enough you write poetry. You stand
limp like an inspiration while our stall
lies unattended. You have the gall—
Her father's got hardscrabble land.
Starve.
Marry for
love." I walked to the door,
saying, "Father, you are, but I am not, a whore."
I strolled out, my nonchalance my dance
bidding goodbye to my inheritance.

## *from* Rebecca and Gabriel's Love Songs for Each Other

### Her *Aubade*

  Pads pawing time, we whirl
after our prey. We lunge and hurl
in for the kill. Our fangs unfurl.
We feed on love. It wolfs our skin.
Dawn knifes apart our lover's dark.

  Dawn flays
the wolf, our dark. The knife, dawn's rays,
pierce and carve the skin. Thrown away,
the wolf corpse slumps, you lit by dawn.
Dawn knifes apart our lover's dark.

  The fur we lose,
the snout grip gone as the dawn's ruse
so riddles us I have no clues
revealing how to save you, wolf—
dawn knifes apart our lover's dark.

  Our death wound, light,
fills our den with morning bright.
My frail young arms are human, slight.
No fangs, no snout, I'm helplessness.
Dawn knifes apart our lovers' dark.

Hurry, my love. The dark's too brief.
Dawn bloodies every twig and leaf.
Hurry. Affirm our wolf belief.
Do not take on your human skin today.
Wolf alive the dawn. Do not go. Stay.

Dawn knifes apart our lover's dark.

## His *Sonnet*

Burnt clove
fragrance and earth within the lips of our
first touch tonight fills this hour
with cries.

Cove,
chicory in dunes, the fall of waves
over me, you, I am the half drowned man who braves
love's ocean inrush,
you.

This loving saves
me from all of what I have been before.

Seas become a falcon,
take me.

Soar.

## Rebecca's Vision at Dawn

Half fallen into lake water, a branch
trails twigs of hieroglyphs,
torn scripture.

A falcon drifts
down to it,
perches
above the water's mirrored calm.

Dawn
births a foal,
easing from the womb,
blood and blind eyes to be licked clean.

The falcon's listening
while the lake diamonds newborn glistening.
I see my death by childbirth—stillborn, my child—and my husband
gone.

A leaf drops.
The mirror shatters.

Helplessness
expands its rings of light and ends where the shores and reeds
begin.

The foal
kicks into life.
It rises, trembling.

Alive.

## Gabriel's Lament

This mule's too weak and cannot take the steep
ascent into the mountain pass. I creep,
leading this tame animal up from the deep.
No trees but wind-ravaged scrub eeks
out along these cliffs and summit rocks.
My father-in-law has land like this, cursed
by drought, driven to wither in death thirst.
No, not this drought torn canyon. This half dead—
In other times, prospering, he would have led.
No, not conquered. Not his hardscrabble stare.
"Whatever happens now, my son, you dare
believe what love has deemed to show you here.
What you have learned from us, beyond all grief,
you must cherish. As for me, I can grieve.
My God, the elder's meeting was beyond belief.
When the high priests appeared, the meeting had
the look of men like wolves gone mad.
A priest like a lawyer decreed the mob
just and good to just go ahead and rob
our temples of their building stone.
Of all the fools and idiots there, I alone
cried, 'Wreck the architecture of our spirit?
Take crowbars? Pry apart our soul and spit
into the yawning emptiness? The gob won't hit
bottom for the year and a day you'll take
mutilating what the Goddess made you make.'
To a man, they mocked me. I am soon dead.
Lucky for you you've got a poet's head.
You take that scholarship from overseas.
Go conquer all those foreign universities."

My mule looks at me long and quizzingly.
It does not know how near or sudden sea
light will break out behind the cliffs and then

its burden's over. We'll climb down to men,
a harbor and the imperialist office where
my papers I'll give over to a nod and stare,
a finger pointing to the ship. Overlords care
enough about their conquered lands to take
a few youth with brains big enough to make
sense of the myths of scientific knowledge.
I have lost all and am off to college.
Who will I meet in the imperial city?
I've taken a vow of lifelong chastity.
Within my dreams, my wife appeared and she
cried, "What's this about a vow? Love, my love.
Go away from your homeland without pity
for yourself. Go walk the years in exile.
Do what you must, but don't defile
love. Love, love well.
Love hard."

Falcon gone with a screech,
she left my arms empty of her. My dreams
bring her soaring to me so that what seems
seems her
alive.

We're climbing down.
The rocks are filling with shrubs. Trees will soon
obscure this skyline's azure afternoon.

Up echoes the
hammering of shipwrights—sails hoisting—
the thriving harbor town.

## The Falcon's Flight

Up here the rivers and the wood
take on the likeness of a wing:
Pinions on pinions vying to
reach and lift
and fling.

Hunting, my eyes are bone,
arrow after arrow driven into stone,
stare of a mummy,
irises gone
to dust.

Of winds using my wings to whirl my
hollow bones into azure sky,
starving flash, I
drop
and grasp
but clutch only empty echoes in the grass.

The sun
rose out of dawn, the light
I obeyed by taking flight.

Immense, cloudless noon
envelopes my wings soaring into the
boon.

# Afterword

1985 Jinzhou, China, was a maze of ancient lanes, twists of crowded one-story brick hovels, with the toilet down the street, with cooking done over a coal stove. Pipes drawing hot exhaust from the coal stoves ran under platforms, called *kangs*, where the family slept, lived and ate. China's modernization, only just beginning, offered five-story ferrous-concrete buildings complete with electricity and running cold water. A cylinder placed under the kitchen sink provided the gas for cooking. An apartment in such a building, highly coveted, only went to party officials, senior faculty members, and my wife and me, the "visiting foreign experts."

We quickly learned to deal with the water and heat shutting on and off during set times every day. Every few days we rode off on our bicycles, going to the market, what Americans would call a farmer's market. At about 1,200 yuan a month, about $200, my and wife's combined salary seems laughable but in 1985 it was ten times what a Jinzhou full professor earned. We could afford luxuries such as bananas and oranges, along with our daily vegetables, eggs and tofu.

The wind, a daily presence, a force, lived up to the local saying, "Jinzhou only has 'big wind' twice a year, each time for six months." Fierce wind rose and set with the sun, gaining strength during the day and, at times, carrying a fine yellow dust. Our city bordered the steppes of inner Mongolia and women often wore scarves over their faces and hair to protect themselves from the wind-borne dust. We arranged our exercise routines around the wind. Behind our apartment building, fields of sorghum and peanuts stretched into the hills and we ran into these hills almost every day. My wife would go after sunrise before the wind became too strong. I would run later, bundled up, heading into the wind and shedding clothes as I ran back, no longer chilled by the headwind, but pushed by a gale-like tailwind.

We taught for two hours a day and had no further duties. I now had time! I devoted myself fully to developing as a poet. For two hours every early morning, Monday through Friday, I sat down and wrote no matter what. For hours, no matter what, I studied the few books I brought from the States. There was no internet making a vast library's worth of literature available. There wasn't even a phone. I had brought collected versions Pound, Williams, Dickinson, Whitman, Chaucer and Shakespeare. I read them for hours every day. For hours, I worked at learning Chinese, both contemporary and classical. Three years of militaristic discipline allowed me, at last, to read the poetry of Li Po in the original. I adhered to this routine with a kind of religious fervor. I began to write publishable poetry by the time I left the country.

Our three years in Jinzhou offered pure and simple peace. The hurly-burly workaholic frenetic life of capitalist society had not yet descended on China. My wife and I settled into a certain rhythm of the sun and wind rising, of the heat and water turning on and off, of cycling to and from the market, of studying and teaching. All the while getting to know our students, colleagues and neighbors. Most evenings we spent alone, studying in our apartment, a habit broken only by dinner invitations, with conversations such as those described in poems "Mr. Mu Zhang Ying." I can only express my gratitude. The Chinese treated us with the greatest generosity and kindness. We were the first Westerners to live in Jinzhou since the Revolution of 1949. We helped to provide a beginning to our college's development. What was a small technical college in 1985, has now become Liaoning Institute of Technology, a major institution of more than ten thousand students. I trust we played a part here, however small.

As our next adventure, we chose Japan's ancient capital. Our lives in Kyoto began with a week-long vacation before searching for work. We ignited, ablaze with joy, touring the ancient capital's temples and gardens. We discovered illimited beauty, green everywhere and shrines on every block, in high contrast to dusty brown Jinzhou, devoid of ornament or any religion whatsoever. We moved from a city with few diversions such as restaurants, movie houses or shops. And we easily found work. Our time in China, a plus in Japanese eyes, the traditional Japanese admiration of China unabated by the terrible and debilitating events of the 20th century that had brought the Middle Kingdom to its knees. Kyoto English Center, a now-defunct English language company, provided us with the sponsorship needed to access both a visa and an apartment. I now found myself taking a train ride everyday to an IBM complex, where I taught seemingly ebullient engineers. In truth they were punch drunk from overwork—fifteen hour work days not uncommon. But they giggled and carried on at the teacher's slightest whimsy. They were fun to teach.

My master's degree, worth far more than it was in the States, allowed me to find employment in the prestigious universities of the Kyoto area. The government allowed university teachers such as myself to work without visa sponsorship, my university contracts considered enough to justify my foreign presence. My visa worries over, freed of the need to work for Kyoto English Center, I now had professor's schedule again and I followed the same militaristic routine I had in China. My study allowed me to deepen my understanding of Li Po while my meandering through the gardens of Kyoto motivated my learning of Buddhism and traditional Japanese aesthetics. My inner life thrived on daily meditation and an ever-deepening awareness of *katachi*, Japanese artistic form. Joy was mine, giving rise to a comic sonnet sequence and other poems celebrating Kyoto. Life was fiery, an ongoing revelation. While I worked on poetry, my wife fell in love with the Japanese language, teaching it to herself. She passed the government's Japanese Proficiency Test at the highest level, which allowed her to attend Japanese university, had she chosen to.

No wonder we stayed for sixteen years. We spent summer vacations cycling throughout the Japanese countryside. Spring vacations had us visiting the countries of southeast Asia. The New Year holiday we reserved for travelling back to the States to remain in contact with our families. We had never planned to stay forever and after many lifetimes of experience we simply left, afraid that the longer we stayed, the more difficult our leaving would be. Fear, as well, undeniably, kept us in Japan for a long time. We had no discernible employment prospects back home and starting over in our forties seemed a daunting prospect.

On returning to the States, my wife and I took a long-planned sabbatical. For eight months, we camped throughout the West's deserts, mountains and shores, along the way making sure to visit lifelong friends made both in Jinzhou and in Irvine, California, during my graduate school years. Upon returning to normal life and with my wife completing her education, I sheltered in an old Victorian rental. I lived like a hermit for about a year, sequestered in my rental's second floor tower room, writing tanka about my sabbatical epiphanic wilderness experiences. I seem to be subject to epiphany or theophany, moments when the radiance of beauty and/or divinity overwhelm my consciousness and I become one with metaphysical energies. I guess perhaps that is one good reason why I write poetry.

We journeyed to Baltimore, Maryland, where my wife and I both found work teaching in the public schools. My wife taught Chinese while I worked for Baltimore County's Home and Hospital division, tutoring students too sick to go to school. I now visit the homes of the sick, working one-on-one and daily experiencing not only a broad wealth of intellectual material but also the broad economic spectrum of my society. In one day I will tutor a millionaire's daughter, drive to a poverty-stricken, single parent household and from there end up in a middleclass townhouse. My politics have turned from moderate Democratic to hardcore left. The waste and degradation offered by our society suffers no excuse. Such deprivation, allowed by our ridiculously old-fashioned constitutional system, means that what was meant for an agrarian society does not suit our industrial, high-tech society. Forty percent of the population controls seventy percent of the Senate, making necessary reforms impossible. The antique two senators-per-state rule of course does not take into account the huge disparities in population caused by our modern system of mega-cities, surrounded by relatively empty rural areas. In truth, the interests of most people are all but unrepresented. And the Senate represents the interests of the wealthy. Both the taxation system and the dispersal of these revenues suffer no excuse. They represent a huge inefficiency and create an enormous demand problem. If the people had more money, more goods and services would be exchanged and the country much wealthier. In every way, a hard dose of socialization would do this country good, including free college and graduate school education for those qualified to be accepted, as well as universal health care. These are hardly radical reforms, being standard in Western Europe, societies not marred by our violence and poverty. Unnecessary suffering results from the United States' non-representative government.

Having now spent more than ten years at my job, teaching all high school levels of English, Social Studies, Science and Math, from the remedial to advanced placement, I have learned a lot, from the contradictions of U.S. history to the ways and means of calculus, discovering early on in my tutoring career my old talent for mathematics, having been given a prize for math at high school graduation. A public school high school degree, if really learned, in truth, is quite an education. And as an auto-didact, knowledge is of course my passion. I am not bragging when I say that I am now, on my own, studying advanced differential equations. And I also am not bragging when I say that I have now, on my own, attained fluency in Latin and am working on a reading knowledge of Ancient Greek. I am pointing out what seems to me necessary for my life as a poet. Continual and lifelong learning gained from both books and experience benefits my ongoing and deepening writing career. Ever since I began to read poetry—I was introduced to it by an unforgettable freshman year teacher named Dr. Anderson—I have had a fierce, burning desire to write poetry. This desire and its expression through writing manifests a sublime and often merciless energy. It is a wildfire that must, without question, be written down. It is a heat and rage, transformed through formal rigor, becoming the beautiful. And these things written down should be as true to the present moment as possible. That is, they should be true to the actual energies of the now demanding expression. They should not be dragged down by the weight of the past. I mean, a poet should have both the ability and the taste to spontaneously choose whatever technique, whether it be some traditional rhyme scheme or prose poem or free verse or whatever, as long as it serves the present's needs. I am really pointing to the dangers of decorum, or, what is considered proper and just, values imposed upon the poem from the outside. Decorum manifests as a time's period style. Just resorting to a technique taken from past experience is a kneejerk response, failing to do justice to the needs of the present moment. And of course the present moment represents what we actually are and how we actually live, however fleeting. My decades of radically disparate experience, brought on both by time and a lot of reading and moving around, has led me to value present-ness.

For realizing this book, endless gratitude I throw at Paul Marion, Keith Finch, Shawn Levy and Juan Delgado.

Irene Somyk, my wife, deserves special thanks. Not I, but she really wrote these poems though she laughs at the very thought.

In memory of my mother, Betty Ann Francis (1928-2022), whose passing a year before this publication issued, prevented me from putting this book in her hands. Let me end with a poem recently written.

## On Entering Old Age

The older I am, the more I
Take in the mirror's gaze
Marbled in folds, lines deepening,
Chiseled in some face

No longer mine but for an art
Long at work to make
A thinker's fist uphold a chin
Cast in bronze, not a fake

Philosophizing but a look
Aware of more than death
When logic fails to affirm love's
Touch. In truth, death is dead.

I should have been an elephant
Cradling a loved one's bones.
My trunk would elongate and lift
Them from dust and stones

To recall why I have trekked far
To what was, kicking dirt
Over the corpse to cover up
One who was, but died first.

I cannot face it. I will die
Alone. The mirror's gaze
Takes in mine as the creme rubs on
And hands, arthritic, shave.

"An isolated couple." Childless.
A blaze of solitude,
Not isolation. We had time
And world enough. I wooed.

Renaissance marble, rebirth's young
Sculptor chiseling and
Finishing love for love— All goes
According to some plan.

    Eternity enfolds us.
Paradise is ours.

If my wife goes first, I will go
Wild, an elephant
Cradling her bones. Death is dead.
There's no such thing as fate.

# Notes on the Poems

Page 15: "A Violent Thunderstorm Caused Me To Drive Right By Emily Dickinson's Gravestone": After attending a wedding in Springfield, MA, I meant to visit Dickinson's grave but was prevented by a torrential downpour.

About 10% of the words are taken from Dickinson's poetry. Of course much is taken from ED #712, but I have used other poems as well, but in these others my use of the language, except for #715, has little or nothing to do with Dickinson's meanings. #715: Hybla balm, Dews of Thessaly, to fetch/#716: undressed/Garter was of gold/#719: a pathos/ of individual voice/ #675: Essential oils/attar, rose/Make summer/ rosemary/#673: smite/Gabriel's wing/ #644: boundaries of pain/ #822: consciousness, adventure, discovery.

17: "For Flaco, The Central Park Zoo's Eagle Owl Escapee": Early winter of 2023, Flaco escaped the Central Park Zoo after his enclosure was cut and vandalized. After being spotted all around Manhattan, the bird settled in Central Park where he feeds upon rats. He surprised his keepers by displaying the ability to hunt, although he had not been taught from birth. The zoo has announced that he can stay free, at least for now. He has achieved both local and internet fame.

19: "The Ancient Romans Believed..." ED#818: "The Thoughtfulness of Thirst".

21-22: "Frailty": The many references to Dickinson's writing are all found in ED#822.

26: "Moth": "Lucifer, the morning star," Isaiah 14:12.

42: "Beetle": "to seek and find," Matthew 7:7-8.

48: "Isaiah": The poem alludes to the 1997 movie *The Ice Storm* in which a dearly loved child is electrocuted by an electric cable downed during an ice storm.

48: "Isaiah": The Winter King, Sir Galahad, Excalibur: From Arthurian legend. The Winter King, a sorcerer, brought eternal winter to the land. No crops could be raised until Sir Galahad took up the great magic sword Excalibur and slew the Winter King, restoring the land to warmth and fertility.

50: "Isaiah": Gulf Sea oil deck. The Gulf of Mexico Disaster, the largest oil spill ever, which occurred on April 20, 2010.

56: "Remembrance": "Flame/Eternal" refers to the everlasting flame installed by John F. Kennedy's gravesite.

59: "The Great Pacific Garbage Patch": see "The Second Coming" by William Butler Yeats.

The Great Pacific Garbage Patch. Estimates put it at 620,000 square miles large, about twice the size of Texas and three times the size of France. It is the hugest of four such ocean garbage patches.

65: "The Ice Storm Hour 5, 11 a.m.": Macbeth, multitudinous, incarnadine: "Will all of Neptune's ocean wash this blood clean from my hand? No, this my hand will rather the multitudinous seas incarnadine, making the green one red." Macbeth Act 2, scene 2.

74: "The Ice Storm Hour 15, 9 p.m.": "Fear not. I bring you tidings of great joy" Luke 2: 10-11.pg. 78: "The Ice Storm Hour 18, Past Midnight": "The frolic architecture of the snow,/Announced by all the trumpets of the sky/Where swan-like forms invest a hidden thorn," lines taken directly from Ralph Waldo Emerson's "The Snow-Storm."

76: "The Ice Storm Hour 18, Past Midnight": mock sun phenomenon. The rising Arctic sun, reflected through ice crystals, creates the illusion of three suns, one on either side of the actual sun.

83: "The Ice Storm Hour 20, 2 a.m.": "the kiln ash" and following, metaphors for aware, Japanese art's emphasis on impermanence and evanescence.

83: "The Ice Storm Hour 21, 3 a.m.": Golgotha, meaning, "The Skull," the place where Jesus of Nazareth suffered crucifixion.

84: "The Ice Storm Hour 21, 3 a.m.": Emmaus. See Luke 24.13-35.

84: "The Ice Storm Hour 22, 4 a.m.": Magdalene. See Mark 16.

85: "The Ice Storm Hour 24, 6 a.m.": these nouns name minerals, gems and alloys.

86: "The Ice Storm Hour 25, 7 a.m.": from the article "Large Scale Dynamics and of the Convection Zone and the Tachocline."

103: "Visiting an Abandoned Buddhist Monastery's Painted Cave": based on a Buddhist story where the Buddha, in a previous life, sacrificed himself to feed a starving tigress and her cubs.

112: "Kyoto Temple Night": The Buddhist tiger represents dignity, perseverance, courage, ferocity. The Buddhist dragon symbolizes enlightenment, the triumph over rage and the growth of wisdom and insight. Further, the Buddhist dragon, as a rain deity, embodies the grace and fertility offered by nature.

116: "The Chupacabra": literally the goat sucker, from American folklore. Sightings are often reported, most notably in Puerto Rico in 1995. The creature is said to prey on goats, sucking their blood dry. Some versions of the myth note that the chupacabra had been a peaceable creature, feeding on flowers, only turning vampirish when the humans destroyed its jungle environment.

122: "Sabi": a term prevalent in Japanese aesthetics, *sabi* is the serenity and simplicity found among the impermanence of things.

128: "By Kyoto's Kamo River, Fox Hunts Down Clown": Japanese fox lore has an ancient history. Red foxes are maleficent trickster spirits out to dupe, possess and even murder hapless mortals. White foxes serve as spirit messengers, delivering wisdom from Inari, the divinity of rice and the harvest. By extension, both Inari and the white foxes express the blessings of plenitude.

130: "Fox's Trail of Cakes Lures Clown into Inari, the Fox Shrine": Fushimi Inari Shrine.

134: "In the Elevator, Clown and Fox Rise": the whirligig of time. See Feste's speech in Twelfth Night, Act 5, Scene 1, lines 372-378.

171: Elephant mourning behavior, such as described here, has been observed and recorded many times.

171: "We had world enough/And time": cf. Marvell's "To his Coy Mistress," line 1, "Had we but world enough and time."

# Acknowledgments

*The Black Fly Review*: An Old Woman Chops Wood

*The Bluffs Reader*: Fox Has Returned to the Top Office

Fox Busily Types

*The Cathartic*: Toward Dawn, a Construction Worker Bulldozes

*Cholla Needles*: A Bat Addresses All of Humanity, On Sleeping in Juan Delgado's Library, Grasshopper, New Mexico Venus So Large It Casts Shadows, Ode to a Chipmunk, Time (Hour 13, 7 P.M. of The Ice Storm)

*Colorado North*: To Become a Buddhist Monk, Clownowl Throws Owl Enters the Garden Where Reigns Kannon, the Goddess of Mercy

*The Connecticut Review:* Kyoto Temple Night

*Connecticut River Review:* The Hummingbird, found in "Three Songs of the Animals"

*Dog River Review*: Fox Dreams (The death moon's black hole bore me. I)

*Folio*: Fox Dreams (Moon's sapphire flames my blood's new rose.)

Clown Dreams (Skinned alive, chicken chortling in)

*The Graham House Review:* Day's End: A Foreigner Jogs into the Fields

*Hollins Critic*: Clown Sees Fox in the Temple Pond's Reflection

*Indigenous Fiction:* The Chupacabra

*Kimera:* The Bear, found in "Three Songs of the Animals"

*The Lowell Review*: Los Angeles Evening

*Nancy's Magazine*: By Kyoto's Kamo River, Fox Hunts Down Clown; Clown, Eventually, Beholds the Trail of Cakes Fox Plunks Down; Fox's Trail of Cakes Lures Clown into Inari, the Fox Shrine

*New Writer's Magazine*: Fox and Clown Wander toward the Temple's Garden Pond

*Omnific*: The Fox God, the Boss, Reviews Clown's Resume

*Pablo Lennis:* Clown's Soul Washes Up on the Shores of Hell's Entrance, Charon's Checking Clown's Credit

*The Pacific Review*: Visiting an Abandoned Buddhist Monastery's Painted Cave, Tanka, At his Daughter's Engagement Feast, Drinking Hard, The Warrior (under the title "The Warrior")

*Paintbrush*: The Falcon's Flight

*Painted Bride Quarterly*: Fox and Clown Enter a Corporate Skyscraper's Lobby, In the Elevator, Clown and Fox Rise

*Pegasus*: Clown's a Fool's Fool's Fool's Fool's Fool's Fool's Fool

*Poem* (U. of Alabama): Fox Gains in Courage, Fox Weeps, Cured of Amnesia

*Slant*: The Dawn Is

*Slipstream*: Mr. Mu Zhang Ying (Parts 1 and 2)

*Small Pond*: They Dream On As One Mind Together

*West Wind Review*: Lynched Crow

# A Note on the Author

Scott Francis lives in Baltimore, Maryland, with his wife, Irene. He works for the Baltimore Country Public Schools' Home and Hospital Division, where he tutors one-on-one high school students too sick to go to school. He helps them keep up with their studies, teaching all levels of language arts, science, math and social studies. He received his M.F.A. from the University of California, Irvine, where he was a Regents Fellow. In 1985 he took a teaching position at Jinzhou Engineering Institute, in northeast China. He and his wife were the first westerners to reside in the city since the Chinese Revoltuion of 1949. There, he composed many of the poems which became the manuscript *Jinzhou 1985 Northeast China*. He also worked hard on learning Ancient Chinese. Three years of study finally allowed him to read, in the original Chinese, the poetry of Li Bai, whose name is also spelled Li Po. In 1988, he moved to the ancient capital of Japan, Kyoto, and began publishing his poetry, eventually placing over two hundred poems in journals such as *The Graham House Review, Paintbrush, Slant* and *Painted Bride Quarterly.* In Kyoto, he worked as an English professor at various institutions including Doshisha University and Kyoto Institute of Foreign Languages. He stayed for sixteen years, composing many uncollected poems as well as a comic book-length sonnet series, *A Dunce Cap Gorged with Kyoto Petrarchan Sonnets*, which was followed by *Lore*, a full-length novelistic work. *Lore* tells the tale of the lives of the Warrior and his family as they struggle to exist in their hunter-gatherer nation newly conquered by an industrialist imperialist power. In 2004, he returned to the United States, taking a yearlong sabbatical, for eight months camping and hiking throughout the southwestern and northwestern mountains, deserts and coastlines. *Wilderness*, a series of tanka-like sequences, commemorates this experience. The author's often satirical responses to his return to his homeland find expression in *Sonnets Broken for America* and *Isaiah*, which is a long poem detailing a ten-year-old's attempts to come to terms with his uncle's death in the Vietnam War. A middle-aged man's struggle to reconcile himself to the demands of his inner life, finds expression in the epic poem, *The Ice Storm*.